The Primary English Class

A PLAY IN TWO ACTS
BY ISRAEL HOROVITZ

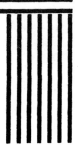

**DRAMATISTS
PLAY SERVICE
INC.**

THE PRIMARY ENGLISH CLASS
Copyright © 1976, Israel Horovitz

All Rights Reserved

SPECIAL NOTE

SPECIAL NOTE ON MUSIC

SPECIAL NOTE ON SONGS AND RECORDINGS

THE PRIMARY ENGLISH CLASS was first presented by Jack Schlissel, Joseph Kipness and Steven Steinlauf at the Circle-in-the-Square Theatre, in New York City, on February 16, 1976. It was directed by Edward Berkeley; the scenery was supervised by Fredda Slaven; lighting was by Andrea Wilson; and the costumes were co-ordinated by Patricia McGourty. The associate producer was Irving Welzer. The cast, in order of appearance, was as follows:

SMIEDNIK	Tom Kubiak
PATUMIERA	Richard Libertini
LaPOUBELLE	Jean-Pierre Stewart
MALE TRANSLATOR	Robert Picardo
MULLEIMER	Sol Frieder
MRS. PONG	Lori Tan Chinn
FEMALE TRANSLATOR	Christine von Dohln
YOKO KUZUKAGO	Atsumi Sakato
DEBBIE WASTBA	Diane Keaton

THE PEOPLE OF THE PLAY
(In the order in which they appear)

SMIEDNIK	A Polish man
PATUMIERA	An Italian man
LaPOUBELLE	A French man
MULLEIMER	A German man
PONG	A Chinese woman
KUZUKAGO	A Japanese woman
WASTBA	An American woman

THE PLACE OF THE PLAY
CLASSROOM

THE TIME OF THE PLAY
NIGHT.

The play is performed with one intermission. The action is continuous.

AUTHOR'S NOTE

I should like to herein gratefully acknowledge the support of The O'Neill Theatre Center, Waterford, Conn., Brandeis University, Waltham, Mass., and The Cubiculo, New York City, where early drafts of *The Primary English Class* were allowed public performance.

Further, I should like to thank Lynne Meadow of The Manhattan Theatre Club, New York, and Paul Libin and Theodore Mann of The Circle in the Square Theatre, New York, for allowing workshop productions of *The Primary English Class* in their theatres, immediately prior to the play's New York premiere.

Finally, I gratefully acknowledge the generous assistance of Martin Esslin, Edith Fournier, Mario Fratti, Eugène Ionesco, Henry Pillsbury, Claude Roy, M. L. Thiersch, Carl Weber, and the performers of each production of *The Primary English Class*, prior to and including its New York premiere production, who enriched, improved and made accurate the various languages of the play, not least of all the English.

I. H., Gloucester, Massachusetts,
September, 1976.

4

For
HENRY PILLSBURY
and
LuANN WALTHER

The Primary English Class

ACT I

NIGHT. *Square box classroom, white plaster walls, wainscoting white as well. Trim color orange. Room reminiscent of handball court: orange lines cut room in court pattern.*

Twelve singular orange student desks, backs of five to Upstage wall, four to Stage-Left wall, three Downstage, between audience and Center Stage.

Small bright orange teacher's desk, Stage-Right wall. Straight-legged variety: teacher's legs and lower trunk constantly exposed to class. Orange wastebasket foot of desk. Wires on Stage-Left wall protrude from small circular cut: clock missing, taken from this spot. Circular shadow visible.

A janitor, Smiednik, is Upstage Left, mopping the floor of the classroom. He is stout, uses regulation-size mop.

In dark, we hear Bulgarian folk music. Then Smiednik sings. Then lights up.

Smiednik sings "I Can't Give You Anything But Love . . . Baby . . ." in Polish. Uses the recognizable melody.*

SMIEDNIK.

Nie mogę, ci dać niczego oprócz *baby*
To jest wszystko co mam, *baby*
Šuij troszeczkę, knuj tioszeczkę
Napewno znajdziesz . . .
Szczęścia i, myśle tak,
Wszystko czego kiedyś chciałeś
Gee, bym cheiał cię widzieć
w bujlautach, *baby*
Tahidi któzych nie ma u Woolworta
Ale dokąd jeszcze nie mozemy, *Baby!*

7

(He stops mopping and gestures as though a nightclub performer in the throes of a big finish.)
Nie mogę ci daċ nic oprócz mnie!
Nie mogę ci daċ nic oprócz, baby!
(In silence now, he straightens row of chairs. Smiednik empties trash can and notices that the clock has been stolen from the wall. He mutters in Polish.)
Psaw krew skradły by buty, gdybym nie uwigzat do nóg. *(He spits.)* Pteww! *(Smiednik gathers his mop into his pail now and goes to door. He opens door and sees that lights are out in the hallway.)* Gdzie do cholery swiatło? *(Pokes head out.)* Ciemno! *(Looks at light in room.)* Gówno! *(Pokes head outside.)* Jest tam kto??? *(No response. He gathers mop and pail again and moves into hallway. Ten count. There is no one on stage. Patumiera enters the room. He believes himself to be a movie-star type. His shirt is silk, open, with a silk ascot, loosely tied. His sunglasses are blue. He carries a black leather briefcase, barristers' variety, plus a second case of the attaché variety, black. He also carries a small black canvas duffel-bag. Several slips of paper are wedged between his teeth and lips. He spins twice in the center of the room, looking for a clock. He tries to lift his arm to look at his own wristwatch, but, due to the weight of his load, he cannot raise his wrist above his waist. He tries twice more and fails twice more. He finally stoops his face to his waist and reads his watch. He mutters, as he closes door to room. He is gasping for breath: winded.)*
PATUMIERA. Chiami un' ambulanza.
TRANSLATOR'S VOICE. Call me an ambulance. *(Patumiera falls into the center chair, D. wall. Thus, he is alone on stage and his back is to the audience. He sits a moment, before muttering again.)*
PATUMIERA. Chiama un dottore.
TRANSLATOR'S VOICE. Call me a doctor. *(He throws his duffel-bag straight U. It lands at the feet of the second student-chair on the U. wall. He throws his black attaché case to the same chair and then he throws his brown briefcase to the same spot. He stands, papers still in mouth, and staggers to the chosen U. wall chair, falls into it, exhausted. He removes his ascot and blue gabardine suitcoat and folds them into his black attaché case. He removes a tangerine from the black duffel-bag, peels it and tries to eat it, but the papers are still in his mouth. He removes them and*

8

eats the tangerine. The door opens and Patumiera wheels around to see who's come into the room. He smiles, assuming he's about to meet his teacher. Mousieur LaPoubelle enters. He is handsome, nearly bald, and diminutive. He wears extremely tight-fitting clothes: gray trousers and a black sweater with a silk scarf at the neck. He carries several papers in his mouth, but at the same time clenches a cigarette between his lips. He carries a cartable-type *French book-satchel on his back and a brown leather briefcase in his left hand. In his right hand, he carries a sport coat and an overcoat and a smashed umbrella. He is also gasping air: winded. He collapses a moment on teacher's desk, causing Patumiera to believe that LaPoubelle is in fact the teacher. Patumiera stands and smiles. LaPoubelle mutters as he closes door.)*

LAPOUBELLE. Appellez une ambulance.

TRANSLATOR'S VOICE. Call me an ambulance.

LAPOUBELLE. Appellez un medecin.

TRANSLATOR'S VOICE. Call me a doctor. *(LaPoubelle staggers to exactly the same* D. *chair first chosen by Patumiera. He drops his load and falls into it.)*

LAPOUBELLE. Merde alors! Zut alors! Fi donc! Bordel!

TRANSLATOR. Crap! Bitch! Damn! Heck!

PATUMIERA. Parla Lei inglese?

TRANSLATOR. You speak English?

LAPOUBELLE. Quoi? . . . Répétez, s'il vous plaît.

PATUMIERA. *(Smiling.)* Parla Lei Eengleesh? *(LaPoubelle stands, drags his load across the room and sits beside Patumiera.)*

LAPOUBELLE. Je comprends un peu.

TRANSLATOR. Yes, I understand a little.

PATUMIERA. Voi siete Francese? Io non parlo. Credo che sono l'unico Italiano nel mondo chi non parla Francese . . .

TRANSLATOR. You're French, right? That's a bad break. I must be the only Italian in the world who doesn't speak a word of French . . .

PATUMIERA. È straordinario quante lingue non parlo.

TRANSLATOR. It's amazing how many languages I don't speak.

PATUMIERA. Italiano è . . . come se dice . . . *tutta.*

TRANSLATOR. Italian is, you might say, *it.*

LAPOUBELLE. Je m'excuse, mais, je suis fatigué . . .

TRANSLATOR. Excuse me, but I'm a little tired . . .

PATUMIERA. (*Grabs LaPoubelle's hand; shakes it.*) Piacere della Sua conoscenza. Il suo nome?
TRANSLATOR. It's a pleasure to meet you. Your name?
LAPOUBELLE. Quoi?
PATUMIERA. Signor Quoi?
LAPOUBELLE. Mister La Poubelle.
PATUMIERA. Non capisco. Scusi.
PATUMIERA. (*Adds with a bit of embarrassment.*) *La Patubelle."*) Je m'appelle Jean-Michel LaPoubelle.
TRANSLATOR. My name is Jean Michel LaPoubelle.
PATUMIERA. (*Taking his hand again.*) Come si chiama, signore?
LAPOUBELLE. Monsieur Chiama, alors?
PATUMIERA. Scusi?
LAPOUBELLE. Vous êtes Meester Chiama, n'est-ce-pas?
PATUMIERA. Meester . . .? (*Laughs.*) Heyyy! No, no, no . . . (*Speaks very slowly indeed.*) Io suo nomo Meester Carlo Fredriko Rizzonini LaPatumiera . . .
TRANSLATOR. My name is Carlo Fredriko Rizzonini LaPatumiera . . .
LAPOUBELLE. Patooo . . . miera?
PATUMIERA. (*Adds with a bit of embarrassment.*) *La* Patumiera.
LAPOUBELLE. (*Smiles.*) Parlez-vous anglais?
PATUMIERA. (*Smiling as well.*) Scusi?
LAPOUBELLE. Excusez-moi. (*Pauses; smiles.*) J'ai complètement oublié . . . (*Speaks in English with an extraordinarily thick accent.*) Do . . . yooo . . . speeks . . . in theee . . . Anglais? (*Patumiera smiles, but does not reply.*) Anglais? (*No reply. Suddenly LaPoubelle slaps his own forehead.*) Non pas *Anglais* . . . c'est *Eeengleesh,* eh? (*Smiles and uses his hands now as he speaks, pantomiming the pulling of each word from his own mouth.*) Do . . . yooo . . . speeks . . . in the Eengleesh?
PATUMIERA. (*Misunderstanding the hand signals for gestures of eating.*) Una morte di fame Io. Qui mangiano solo roba da animali. Roba che ti distrugge il cervello. Buona per porci, forse. Non di certo per la gente!
TRANSLATOR. I'll say I'm hungry. All they eat here is animal food. It destroys the brain. Fit for pigs not people.
PATUMIERA. Ho ordinato una pastasciutta, giu . . . Cosi spappolata da restar tutta attaccata alla parete.

TRANSLATOR. I ordered a pasta downstairs . . .. for snack . . . It was so overcooked, it stuck to the wall.

PATUMIERA. Non credo che siano stati contenti del fatta che l'ho sbattuta contro la parete ma . . .

TRANSLATOR. Hey, I don't think they appreciated me throwing it against the wall, but . . .

LAPOUBELLE. (*After a long pause.*) Dooo . . . yooo . . . speeks in the Eeengleesh?

PATUMIERA. Eeengleesh?

LAPOUBELLE. C'est quoi? Ce n'est pas "Eeengleesh?" (*Slaps head; laughs.*) Ahhh-oui! (*Corrects himself.*) C'est *Ahhng-leesh* . . .

PATUMIERA. (*Smiling.*) C'est? (*Confused.*) Enngleesh? (*Recognizes word; he laughs.*) Ah! Si! Si si! Si si si! *Eeengleesh!* (*Silence.*)

LAPOUBELLE. I . . . habit . . . à . . . from . . . Paris . . . up unteel . . . *Merde!*

PATUMIERA. Merda? (*LaPoubelle opens briefcase; finds French/ English dictionary, begins to look for words.*)

LAPOUBELLE. Excusez-moi, cher Monsieur Patchuli . . .

PATUMIERA. Patumiera!

LAPOUBELLE. (*Looking up; slightly annoyed.*) Ah, oui, bien, sûr . . . Patoo . . .

PATUMIERA. . . . eee—air—rah . . . Patumiera . . .

LAPOUBELLE. Oui. Bon.

PATUMIERA. Le piacciono le pellicole americane?

TRANSLATOR. Do you like American movies?

LAPOUBELLE. Qu'est-ce que vous avez dit?

TRANSLATOR. What did you say?

PATUMIERA. (*Pauses.*) . . . non si preoccupi! (*He rushes to his desk, opens briefcase and grabs his Italian/English dictionary.*)

LAPOUBELLE. (*Searching in his dictionary.*) Une seconde . . . (*Reading.*) Hibou . . . hic . . . hideux . . . ben, merde, alors! . . . (*Finds his words.*) Ahhh-oui! Hier! (*Reads.*) Yez-ter-dai . . . (*Corrects himself.*) Yester . . . dayii . . .

PATUMIERA. (*Smiling, doesn't look up from his own dictionary.*) Aspeta momento . . .

LAPOUBELLE. (*Suddenly angry.*) Merde alors! Fi donc! Zut alors! Bordel!

PATUMIERA. Che è successo?

LAPOUBELLE. (*Explaining, in French.*) Ce n'est pas *yester-quoi*
. . . vous savez . . .

PATUMIERA. Uno momento!

LAPOUBELLE. C'est avant hier . . .

PATUMIERA. Uno momento.

LAPOUBELLE. . . . non pas hier!

PATUMIERA. (*Looks up and smiles again.*) Non si preoccupi,
eh? (*Back into his dictionary again.*)

LAPOUBELLE. (*Screams.*) Regardez-moi! Je veux qu'on s'occupe
de moi!

PATUMIERA. (*Angrily.*) Basta!

LAPOUBELLE. Basta?

PATUMIERA. Basta!

LAPOUBELLE. (*Not laughing now, but instead quizzical.*) Basta?

PATUMIERA. (*Simply; confused.*) Si, basta.

LAPOUBELLE. Je connais le mot *basta*. C'est italien, alors!

TRANSLATOR. I know the word *basta*. It's Italian, right?

PATUMIERA. (*Ashamed of himself now.*) Si, basta. (*Shrugs.*)
Scusi, eh?

LAPOUBELLE. C'est certainement italien . . . (*Smiles.*) Vous
êtes italien?

PATUMIERA. Italien?

LAPOUBELLE. Oui, oui. Vous. Italien?

PATUMIERA. (*Realizes he is finally understood. Very pleased.*)
Si. Si si. Si si si. (*Laughing and smiling. He shakes LaPoubelle's
hand again.*) Mi chiamo Carlo Fredriko Rizzonini LaPatumiera
. . . (*Smiles; leans back. Smiles again.*) Come si chiama, signor?
(*There is a long pause.*)

LAPOUBELLE. Incroyable. Je parle anglais mieux que je parle
italien.

TRANSLATOR. Incredible. I speak English better than I speak
Italian.

PATUMIERA. Scusi?

LAPOUBELLE. Scusi? Je fais trois mille kolometer pour me
trouver en face d'un plat de ravioli.

TRANSLATOR. I have to travel three thousand miles to end up
in a room with a plate of ravioli.

PATUMIERA. Scusi?

LAPOUBELLE. Je dois être le seul Français au monde qui ne parle aucune autre langue. Que la sienne—c'est notre tare familiale. Les langues . . .

TRANSLATOR. I must be the only Frenchman in the world who speaks absolutely no other language than French. Language is my family curse. (*Patumiera is working at dictionary and phrasebook.*)

LAPOUBELLE. Je suis désolé d'avoir crié. Vraiment. Ce n'est pas dans mes habitudes. Pas du tout. Je suis en fait un type tranquil.

TRANSLATOR'S VOICE. I'm sorry I yelled. I really am. It's not like me. Not at all. I'm really a quiet guy.

LAPOUBELLE. La vérité c'est que je suis plutôt bien connu . . . pour être tranquil.

TRANSLATOR'S VOICE. The fact of the matter is, I'm rather well known . . . for being quiet.

LAPOUBELLE. Je dois avoir des soucis.

TRANSLATOR'S VOICE. I must be anxious.

LAPOUBELLE. Evidement j'ai des soucis! Qui n'en aurait pas à ma place?

TRANSLATOR'S VOICE. Of course I'm anxious! Who wouldn't be?

LAPOUBELLE. Se taper six étages et dans le noir en plus! Mais qu'est-ce qu'elles ont, ces fichues lumières?

TRANSLATOR'S VOICE. Climbing a million stairs in pitch black What the hell's the matter with the lights out there?

LAPOUBELLE. Je crois qu'on vient de m'empoisonner. En bas. J'ai commandé et mangé un petit bout de saucisson. Pour boucher un trou. Comme nourriture, ça avait l'air d'être destiné à notre ami le cochon plutôt que d'en provenir.

TRANSLATOR'S VOICE. I think I was poisoned just now. Downstairs. I ordered and ate a little drop of sausage . . . for a snack . . . It wasn't food *from* our friend, the pig, it was food *for* our friend the pig!

LAPOUBELLE. Mon estomac fait de ces bruits impardonables. Je suis absolument navré.

TRANSLATOR'S VOICE. My stomach is making unforgivable sounds. I am desperately sorry. (*Patumiera suddenly throws down his dictionary after scratching forever on a piece of paper. He extends his arms, as if to say, "Now, I understand." LaPoubelle takes Patumiera's gesture to mean "Now, I understand." LaPoubelle smiles.*)

PATUMIERA. (*With an enormous smile on his face and notes in hand.*) Dooo . . . yooo . . . liiiike . . . Ahhmerican . . . mooo-fies?

LAPOUBELLE. Je ne comprends pas?

PATUMIERA. (*Pulling each word from his mouth; speaks extraordinarily slowly.*) Dooo . . . yooo . . . liiiike . . . Ahmerican moo-fies?

LAPOUBELLE. (*Still thinks Patumiera is commenting on his illness.*) Oui, j'ai mai à l'estomac . . . C'est affreux . . .

TRANSLATOR. Yes, I've got an awful bellyache.

PATUMIERA. (*Tries again, still smiling. This time he offers LaPoubelle an 8x10 glossy resume photograph of himself, which Patumiera holds next to his own face, for comparison.*) Dooo . . . yooo . . . liiiike . . . Ahmerican mofies? (*Smiles more than ever.*) Ahhh dooo lotz. (*LaPoubelle takes Patumiera's 8x10 glossy photograph from him, comparing the man and the face. Patumiera takes LaPoubelle's pen.*) Ha lei una penna?

LAPOUBELLE. La stylo . . . ? Oui, s'il vous plaît? (*LaPoubelle looks at photo, smiles. Patumiera takes back photo and autographs same and hands it back to LaPoubelle who looks at same and laughs. Patumiera pockets LaPoubelle's pen*) . . . mon cher Monsieur . . . Ah, ma stylo. (*Patumiera gives back pen to Lapoubelle, who is laughing out of control now.*) C'est drôle!

PATUMIERA. (*Grabbing photograph away from LaPoubelle.*) Che è successo?

TRANSLATOR. What's going on?

LAPOUBELLE. (*Laughing still out of control.*) Mon Dieu! (*Doubled over.*) Ma tête! (*Leaning on his desk.*) Excusez-moi, cher monsieur . . . c'est drôle, hein?

PATUMIERA. (*Angrily.*) Basta! Questa è la mia faccia a tu stai ridendo, biscotti.

TRANSLATOR. That's my face you're laughing at, cupcake.

LAPOUBELLE. Ca va, bien. Tien! (*Pauses.*) Que j'ai mal à la tête! Mais mon Dieu! (*Turns to Patumiera again.*) Il faut que nous speekons thee Eenglish now, hein? (*Thumbs through his dictionary.*) Ecoutez! Yooo haf . . . how many . . . years?

PATUMIERA. Non capisco. Scusi. (*His feelings are hurt.*)

LAPOUBELLE. (*Repeats himself, but slowly.*) Yoo haf . . . how many years?

PATUMIERA. Non capisco. Scusi. (*Paces; refuses to answer. His feelings are still hurt.*)

14

LAPOUBELLE. (*Angry now.*) "Non capisco. Non capisco." C'est tout ce que vous savez dire? "Non capisco."
PATUMIERA. Calma, calma, Signor Pooblini . . .
LAPOUBELLE. Poubelle . . . LaPoubelle. Je m'appelle LaPoubelle. C'est facile, LaPoubelle! Vous voulez voir! (*LaPoubelle walks to the wastebasket that is positioned at front left leg of teacher's desk. He lifts wastebasket and waves it in Patumiera's face.*) Regardez mon nom! LaPoubelle. Oui-oui, je sais. (*Shrugs. Sets down wastebasket.*) C'est exactement le même mot: LaPoubelle. C'est ne pas banal, hein?
PATUMIERA. (*Extremely confused now.*) Scusi . . . (*Shrugs.*) Non capisco . . . (*Holds up hands so as to not be yelled at by LaPoubelle.*) I suo nome LAPOUBELLE? (*Smiles and picks up wastebasket.*) Mi chiamo la Patumiera . . . (*No reply; louder.*) Io sono Carlo Fredriko Rizzonini La Patumiera . . . (*Waves wastebasket.*) La Patumiera! (*LaPoubelle begins to understand. Points to wastebasket.*)
LAPOUBELLE. Patumier . . . quoi?
PATUMIERA. Patumiera. (*Begins to realize.*) LaPoubelle?
LAPOUBELLE. Oui, LaPoubelle!
PATUMIERA. LaPoubelle?
LAPOUBELLE. Patumiera? (*They both laugh now, understanding that they share the same name. They embrace, clapping each other's back. LaPoubelle sets wastebasket down again on its proper spot as they continue to laugh and point to wastebasket time and time again, stretching the moment out as long as they can before they fall again into embarrassed silence. They return to their seats. Each begins to thumb through his dictionary. New man enters, Mulleimer. He is dressed in grey slacks, black blazer with club patch, white shirt, striped tie, maroon sleeveless vest-sweater underneath jacket. He carries several briefcases and sacks. He wears incredibly thick eyeglasses. He holds papers in his mouth. Two cameras are strapped across his chest. He wears a raincoat over all, which he will soon try to remove without first removing cameras. He is totally breathless. He leans upon teacher's desk in state of near-collapse, attempting to regain normal breathing. Both LaPoubelle and Patumiera assume that Mulleimer is the teacher, because he is at teacher's desk. They stand behind their desks and smile at Mulleimer, who finally notices them and speaks, smiling as well.*)

MULLEIMER. Ach du liebe Scheisse! (*Collapses into chair.*) Ach du liebe heilige Scheisse! (*Throws his briefcase on floor.*) Ich krieg noch einen Herzschlag! (*Heaves his chest.*) Ich glaube ich hab' einen Herz Anfall!

TRANSLATOR. Holy crap! Holy jumping crap! I'm having a heart attack! I think I'm in coronary arrest!

MULLEIMER. Warum brennen denn die Lampen draussen nicht? Bin doch Kein Kananchen, ha, ha!

TRANSLATOR. Why the hell are the lights out out there? I'm not a rabbit!

MULLEIMER. (*Looks at other men.*) Was ist denn für eine beschissene Schule hier? Sechs Treppen hoch und Kein Fahrstuhl!

TRANSLATOR. What the hell kind of a school is this anyway? Six flights up and no elevator!

MULLEIMER. Für was halten die uns?

TRANSLATOR. What do they take us for?

MULLEIMER. Kancgeruhs? (*Laughs at his own joke.*) Hah-hah-hah! (*Pauses; notices other men staring. Checks his fly zipper.*) Was glotzen Sie mich denn so an?

TRANSLATOR. What are you staring at?

MULLEIMER. Haben Sie noch nie jemand mit einer Brille gesehen?

TRANSLATOR. Haven't you ever seen a man with eyeglasses before?

LAPOUBELLE. Qui êtes-vous?

TRANSLATOR. Who are you?

PATUMIERA. Credo di essere nella stanza sbagliata. (*Stands; smiles to LaPoubelle.*)

TRANSLATOR. I think I'm in the wrong room.

PATUMIERA. Credo di essere nella classe sbagliata. (*Gathers his many briefcases and papers.*) Fottiti, piscione! (*Walks to door. Looks at number on door. Looks at paper in teeth.*) Il numero e' lo stesso.

TRANSLATOR. The number's the same.

MULLEIMER. Tut mir leid, aber ich spreche kein Englisch.

TRANSLATOR. Sorry, but I don't speak any English.

PATUMIERA. Che hai detto?

MULLEIMER. Das ist doch nicht Englisch.

TRANSLATOR. That's not English.

PATUMIERA. Credevo che questa fosse la classe per l'Inglese elementare.

TRANSLATOR. I thought that this was the Primary English Class.

MULLEIMER. Mir Klingt das mehr wie Spanisch.

TRANSLATOR. That sounds like Spanish to me.

PATUMIERA. Sono nella stanza sbagliata. Scusi.

TRANSLATOR. I'm in the wrong room. Excuse me. (*It is here that Mulleimer begins to entangle himself in his raincoat, which he has tried to remove without first removing the cameras that are strapped across his chest.*)

MULLEIMER. Ich glaub' ich hab' mich in Zimmer geirrt. Entschuldigung.

TRANSLATOR. I'm in the wrong room. Excuse me.

LAPOUBELLE. (*Stands.*) Ca m'étonne que ça m'arrive à moi, mais il me semble que je me suis trompé de salle. Sacre bleu!

TRANSLATOR. I'm in the wrong room. Excuse me. (*They all crowd to the door. They all exit and the stage is absolutely empty for a count of ten. LaPoubelle is first to return.*)

LAPOUBELLE. Moi, j'ai raison, eux, ils ont tort.

TRANSLATOR. I'm right, they're wrong.

PATUMIERA. (*Enters quickly, smiling.*) Io ho ragione, loro hanno torto.

TRANSLATOR. I'm right, they're wrong.

MULLEIMER. (*Enters scratching head.*) Ich hab'recht, Sie nicht.

TRANSLATOR. I'm right: you're wrong.

PATUMIERA. Alemno ci sta la luce. Un po basso ma la luce.

TRANSLATOR. At least the lights are on. Dim, but on.

MULLEIMER. Wenigstens brennen die Lampen wieder, Trübe, aber doch.

TRANSLATOR. At least the lights are on. Dim, but on.

LAPOUBELLE. Au moins il y a de la lumière. Pas beaucoup, mais enfin.

TRANSLATOR. At least the lights are on. Dim, but on.

LAPOUBELLE. Je 'mexcuse, mais je ne parle pas norvègien.

TRANSLATOR. Excuse me, I don't speak Norwegian.

PATUMIERA. Mi dispiace, ma non parlo olandese.

TRANSLATOR. Excuse me, I don't speak Dutch.

MULLEIMER. Tut mir leid, aber ich spreche weder Flamisch noch Portugiesisch . . . Spreche auch weder Franzoesisch, Englisch, Italienisch, Griechisch noch Hebraeisch.

TRANSLATOR. Excuse me, I don't speak either Flemish or Portuguese. I can't speak French, Italian, English, Greek or Hebrew, either.
MULLEIMER. Meine einzige Zunge ist und bleibt Deutsch.
TRANSLATOR. Actually, German's just about it for me. (*They all sit. Smile. Silence.*)
MULLEIMER. Mein Namme ist Mülleimer. (*He picks up and points to wastebasket as he says his name.*)
TRANSLATOR. My name is Mülleimer.
MULLEIMER. Fritz Mülleimer.
LAPOUBELLE. (*Looks at wastebasket and then waves casually to Mulleimer.*) Oui, oui, je m'appelle LaPoubelle.
PATUMIERA. (*Looks at wastebasket at same time and also waves casually to Mulleimer.*) Si, si. Io sono la Patumiera . . . (*Smiles across to LaPoubelle.*) Si, si si, si si si. La Poubelle!
LAPOUBELLE. (*Smiles across to Patumiera.*) Oui, oui oui, oui oui oui. La Patumiera, aussi!
MULLEIMER. (*Smiling into his confusion.*) Ja. Ja-ja. Ja-ja-ja. (*Pauses: sets basket down.*) Wie, bitte?
LAPOUBELLE. Comment vous appellez-vous? Je m'appelle La-Poubelle. (*LaPoubelle and Mulleimer smile at one another. After a long pause, Patumiera speaks, English phrasebook in hands. Waving to indicate that the room is warm.*)
PATUMIERA. (*In English.*) I . . . canno breth. I . . . canno breth . . . (*Smiles. He offers a raisin to Mulleimer and LaPoubelle after reading word on box.*) Want uno ray-zeen?
MULLEIMER. Nein danke, *and* LAPOUBELLE. Non, Merci. bin satt. J'en ai jusque là . . .
TRANSLATOR. No thanks, TRANSLATOR. No, thank stuffed. you. Stuffed.
(*Patumiera waves his arm again to indicate that it is warm in the room. He repeats his newly learned English idiom.*) I . . . canno . . . breth . . . (*He is gaily popping raisins into his mouth. LaPoubelle repeats his last word, in English.*)
LAPOUBELLE. Breth? . . . (*LaPoubelle begins to look for word in his French/English dictionary.*) Breth? . . . Je chercherai . . .
TRANSLATOR. Breth? I'll look it up. (*A raisin lodges in Patumiera's throat. He chokes. He will begin now to make incredible sounds, wheezes and groans. He will whack his own back, crawl*

about the floor near his desk, flail his arms and his face will become bright red in color. No one will pay close attention.)
MULLEIMER. *(Interrupting LaPoubelle's dictionary search.)* Es tut mir Leid, aber ich spreche kein Portugiesisch. *(LaPoubelle looks up absently at Mulleimer, who is standing next to him, smiling broadly.)*
LAPOUBELLE. Comment?
MULLEIMER. Es tut mir Leid, aber ich spreche kein Portugiesisch.
TRANSLATOR. I'm sorry, but I don't speak Portuguese.
LAPOUBELLE. *(Takes phrasebook.)* Vous permettez, s'il vous plait? I . . . canno' breth, eh? Breth?
PATUMIERA. *(Reads as he chokes. Repeats in English.)* I . . . canno . . . breth . . .
LAPOUBELLE. Breth, eh? Ça va. D'accord. Je chercherai . . .
TRANSLATOR. "Breth," huh? Okay, then. I'll look it up . . .
MULLEIMER. Das ist doch die Anfängerklasse für Englisch hier, ja?
TRANSLATOR. This is the primary English class, right?
MULLEIMER. *(After no response.)* Kann hier denn keiner sprechen?
TRANSLATOR. Well, how come nobody knows how to talk in here? *(No response. LaPoubelle is busily looking up the word "Breth" in his dictionary. Patumiera is whacking himself on the back and dying. Mulleimer, cleaning his glasses, sees nothing.)*
MULLEIMER. Sie müssen wissen Ich habe fast zehn Jahre gespart, un hier herzukommen . . . in dieses Land.
TRANSLATOR. I'd like you to know that I saved my money nearly ten years to come here . . . to this country.
MULLEIMER. Und Unterwegs wäre ich beinahe umgebracht worden, im Flugzeug. Von einem Luft-Piraten.
TRANSLATOR. And I nearly got killed on the airplane coming here. By a highjacker.
MULLEIMER. Auf der Untergrundbahn wär ich auch beinahe umgebracht worden. *(Pauses.)*
TRANSLATOR. I almost got killed on the subway, too. *(Patumiera continues to choke and babble in Italian, calling for help.)*
MULLEIMER. Auch von einem Piraten. *(Pauses.)*
TRANSLATOR. Also by a highjacker.

19

MULLEIMER. In Hotel-Fahrstuhl wär ich auch beinahe umge-
bracht worden. (Pauses.)
TRANSLATOR. I almost got killed in my hotel elevator too.
MULLEIMER. Nicht von einem Luft-Piraten. Was zum Tuefel
hätte auch ein Luft-Pirat in einem Hotel-Fahrstuhl zu suchen?
(Pauses.)
TRANSLATOR. Not by a highjacker. What the hell would a
highjacker do with a hotel elevator?
MULLEIMER. Das war ein "Mugger" im Fahrstuhl. (Pauses.)
TRANSLATOR. (German accent on word "mugger.") There was
a "mugger" in the elevator.
MULLEIMER. Zu meinem Gluck war er unglaubich alt. (Pauses,
no reply.)
TRANSLATOR. Lucky for me, he was incredibly old.
MULLEIMER. Heiss hier drinnen. (Pauses.)
TRANSLATOR. It's hot in here.
MULLEIMER. Ich krieg keine Luft.
TRANSLATOR. I can not breathe.
LAPOUBELLE. I canno . . . breathe?
PATUMIERA. Si. Si si. Si si si.
LAPOUBELLE. Comment?
PATUMIERA. Non posso respirare.
LAPOUBELLE. Je ne peux rien trouver de pareil dans mon
dictionnaire.
TRANSLATOR'S VOICE. I can't find anything like that in my
dictionary.
LAPOUBELLE. Tout ce que je trouve de semblable c'est le mot
"respirer."
TRANSLATOR'S VOICE. All I can find that's close is the word
"breathe."
LAPOUBELLE. Mais, si vous ne pouviez pas respirer depuis la
première fois que vous avez dit "Je ne peux pas respirer" . . .
TRANSLATOR'S VOICE. But, if you couldn't breath since the
first time you said "I cannot breathe" . . .
LAPOUBELLE. . . . vous seriez . . . ben . . . mort.
TRANSLATOR'S VOICE. . . . You'd be . . . well . . . dead.
(Patumiera begins choking violently.)
LAPOUBELLE. Ca suffit cinema! Qu'est-ce qu'il y a?
TRANSLATOR. You're making a fool of yourself! What is it?

MULLEIMER. Sie machen sich ja laecherlich. Was haben Sie denn eigentlich?

TRANSLATOR. You're making a fool of yourself! What is it?

PATUMERIA. One canno . . . *breathe!* Non si respira un cavolo qui! (*Patumiera coughs violently and the raisin is released. LaPoubelle and Mulleimer whack him on the back several times until it looks as though they are killing him. Small old Chinese woman enters, watches, sits. She is absolutely silent.*) Cosi e' maglio! (*Patumiera stops coughing, but men have now lifted him on to teacher's desk and continue whacking his back.*) Basta! Basta! (*They stop. Patumiera is furious that they have overwhacked him. He first punches LaPoubelle's arm, as he smiles and says "Grazie."*) Grazie! (*He now punches Mulleimer's arm.*) Grazie tanto! (*Mulleimer rolls with the punch and is the first to notice the old Chinese woman, Mrs. Pong.*)

MULLEIMER. Ach! Guckt mal! Guten Abend, gnädige Frau . . . (*He bows slightly, clicking his heels.*)

LAPOUBELLE. Bonsoir, madame . . . (*He bows.*)

PATUMIERA. Bouna sera, signora . . . (*He kisses her hand.*)

MRS. PONG. Nay how mah?

LAPOUBELLE. Vous êtes japonaise?

MRS. PONG. M goi nā, ngoi m sät yĭt gä fŏn wah wä . . .

TRANSLATOR'S VOICE. Excuse me, but I don't even speak a word of English . . .

MRS. PONG. Gĭm mŏn hai ngoi gä ai yĭt ngĭt ŏw coi gä fai wä.

TRANSLATOR'S VOICE. This is my very first day in the city . . .

MRS. PONG. Ngoi dieng-ä loi may gŏk dŏm mŏn sē yä.

TRANSLATOR'S VOICE. I just got to this country yesterday . . .

MRS. PONG. Säle-lë . . .

TRANSLATOR'S VOICE. Sorry. (*The three men have been standing, staring at Mrs. Pong as she spoke. They are astonished. LaPoubelle is first to speak, as he goes to his desk and sits.*)

LAPOUBELLE. Merde.

PATUMIERA. Merda.

MULLEIMER. Scheisse. (*Silence. A beautiful young Japanese woman enters, Yoko Kuzukago. She smiles and bows at EVERY-ONE. Then she places a red apple on teacher's desk and giggles. She is breathing deeply, trying to catch her breath. She carries several small canvas bags, filled with books and papers. She has papers between her teeth.*)

LAPOUBELLE. Bonjour, ma jolie . . . (*LaPoubelle bows and smiles.*)

MULLEIMER. Guten Abend, mein Schatz. (*Mulleimer bows and clicks heels and smiles.*)

PATUMIERA. Ebbene, ciao, tesoro . . . (*Patumiera straightens his spine and sucks in his stomach and smiles. Yoko giggles copiously. LaPoubelle takes her hand and kisses it. Patumiera moves in as a movie star might and takes her hand. By mistake, he actually finds that he has taken LaPoubelle's hand and is about to kiss same. Patumiera hurls LaPoubelle's hand away and takes Yoko's hand, which he now kisses deeply, using his tongue for emphasis. Yoko giggles copious giggles.*) Ah, tesoro . . . Tesoro mio . . .

YOKO. Daibu okure mashitaka? Ichijikan hodo maeni kitemimashitaga makkura deshita. Sorede shitano chisana resutoran de karui shokuji o shite kimashita.

TRANSLATOR. Am I terribly late? I stopped here about an hour ago, but all the lights were out, so I stopped at the little restaurant downstairs and had a bite.

YOKO. I no choshi ga chotto hendesu.

TRANSLATOR. I feel a little sick to my stomach.

LAPOUBELLE. Excusez-moi?

YOKO. Sukunakutomo akari ga tsuiteimasune. Kurai kedo tonikaku.

TRANSLATOR. At least the lights are on. Dim, but on.

PATUMIERA. (*Ushering Yoko to seat beside his.*) Mia cara signorina, nelle poche ore da me vissute in America, ho gia' visto, letteralmente, milioni di donne. Ma lei e chiaramente la pui belle di tutte. Che Dio la benedica.

TRANSLATOR. My dear young lady, in the scant 36 hours in which I've lived here in America, I have already looked at literally millions of women. But you are clearly the most beautiful of them all. God bless you.

YOKO. (*She turns to Patumiera, giggling.*) Sumimasenga anatano osshatteiru kotoga wakarimasen.

TRANSLATOR. I'm sorry, but I don't understand you.

PATUMIERA. (*Confused.*) Scusi?

MULLEIMER. (*Grabs Yoko, tries to lure her away from Patumiera.*) Meine name ist Mülleimer.

YOKO. Hai. Hai hai. Hai hai hai. (*Pauses.*) Moshiwake arimasenga eigoga hanasemasen. (*Smiles and bows.*)

TRANSLATOR. Yes. Yes, yes. Yes, yes, yes. Sorry, but I don't speak a word of English.

MULLEIMER. (Confused.) Gefällt ihnen denn mein Name nicht? Das wündert mich aber sehr.

TRANSLATOR. You think my name is funny? Well, who doesn't?

LAPOUBELLE. (Smiling broadly.) Vous êtes Chinoise? (Patumiera moves behind Yoko with air of great secrecy. He puts his fingers to his lips, as he whispers to her.)

PATUMIERA. Ho un segreto, Io!

TRANSLATOR. I have a secret!

PATUMIERA. Sono un membro del partito comunista.

TRANSLATOR. I am a member of the Communist Party.

MULLEIMER. (Points to wastebasket.) Weiss schon, die Leute machen sich immer über meinen Namen lustig.

TRANSLATOR. People always laugh at the obvious, I know.

LAPOUBELLE. (Sees Mulleimer pointing at wastebasket.) C'est drôle, n'est-ce pas? Je sais, je sais.

TRANSLATOR. It's funny, isn't it? I know. I know.

MULLEIMER. Darf ich mich vorstellen, meine Fraulein . . . (Extends his hand, leaning to her.) Meine name ist Mülleimer.

YOKO. Hajimemashite.

LAPOUBELLE. (Leans in as well.) Je m'appelle LaPoubelle . . .

YOKO. Hajimemashite.

PATUMIERA. La Patumiera . . . (All are amazed to discover they all share common name.)

YOKO. Watashi no namaewa Kuzukago Yoko desu. (She points to wastebasket.)

TRANSLATOR. My name is Yoko Kuzukago.

YOKO. Kuzukago Yoko. Kuzukago Yoko. (All are smiling into each other's eyes as old Chinese woman moans, pitches forward out of her chair in a faint. Yoko is first to scream.) Ta-i-hen!

PATUMIERA. Madonna mia!

MULLEIMER. Mein Gott!

LAPOUBELLE. Mon. Dieu! De l'eau! (He exits the room.)

TRANSLATOR. Water!

MULLEIMER. Wasser! (He exits the room.)

TRANSLATOR. Water!

PATUMIERA. Acqua! (He exits the room.)

TRANSLATOR. Water!

YOKO. Ocha!

TRANSLATOR. Tea! (*Yoko also exits the room and, for a moment, the old Chinese woman is alone, on the floor. Slowly, she pulls herself over to her chair and, holding it for support, stands. She shakes her head. She sits in the chair, composed again. An American woman, Debbie Wastba, enters. She is laden with bookbags, shopping bags, handbags and briefcases: all hers. She has papers in her teeth. She is out of breath. She wears a long trenchcoat, British, with a colorful scarf, French. Her shoes are Italian and her bookbags a blend of Japanese, German and Chinese. Her clothing is probably a skirt and blouse, slightly subdued, perhaps with black tights worn under the skirt. Her clothing gives her an air of competence. She looks about the empty room, seeing the many bookbags, attaché cases, jackets, etc. Finally, she sees the old Chinese woman, Mrs. Pong, and smiles broadly.*)

WASTBA. Hi. I'm Ms. Wastba. (*Pronounced "Wah-stah-bah."*) Odd name, huh? Dates all the way back to Mesopotamia. Wastba. (*Spells it.*) W-A-S-T-B-A. (*Pauses.*) My great grandfather shortened it . . . after his . . . uh . . . trouble. (*Pauses.*) Some muggy night, huh? I can't breathe. (*Pauses. Fanning the air.*) I've never been able to take heat, which is ridiculous, when you consider my family background. Three thousand years of rotten luck. All we had to do was stay put and we would have been swimming in gas and oil, but, no, we moved on and here I am. After six flights of climbing, I'd hate to be standing next to me on a bus. (*Laughs a bit at her own joke.*) Ah, yes . . . (*Sets down a bag or two.*) Wouldn't you know the elevator would be on the fritz? That's a slang word: fritz. (*Pauses.*) You don't speak English at all, huh? (*Pauses; laughs.*) I forgot. That's why you're here. (*She laughs again.*) No English at all? (*No response.*) That's okay, really. Listen, that's all the better. No rotten habits, you know what I mean? (*Pauses; smiles, unpacking her notebooks.*) This is going to be total immersion. (*Smiles.*) Total. (*Pauses; smiles again.*) That means no speaking your base language. Which would certainly be Oriental in your case, right? (*Pauses, looks around room and sees men's bags and clothes in room.*) You sure brought a lot of stuff, didn't you? (*Pauses.*) There should be more of us. Maybe they're all late. (*Looks for clock; sees wires.*) There must be a clock . . . Look at that! Clock's been stolen. (*Shakes her head to express "What's the use?", as she unpacks more books.*) They'll steal anything nowadays, really. An old gentleman I know . . . *quite* well . . . he had his doorknobs taken. (*Pauses.*) It's true. Hard to believe, isn't it? (*Pauses.*) Listen, he was relieved they didn't get into his apartment altogether. (*Smiles.*) Of course, neither did he . . . not for hours. (*Giggles a bit; explains.*) No knobs. (*Pauses.*) At the time, I thought it was kind of . . . well . . . kinky . . . *You* might say "inscrutable," right? (*She laughs. No response from Pong. LaPoubelle rushes into room carrying a take-out container of water. He rushes to Mrs. Pong.*)

LAPOUBELLE. Voici. De l'eau! Pour vous . . . Buvez un coup . . . Ca ira mieux . . . Buvez, buvez, etc. . . . (*Patumiera, the same. Offers container.*)

PATUMIERA. Acqua per lei, signora. (*And he bends near Mrs. Pong, forcing her to drink as he babbles encouraging phrases. Mulleimer rushes into room, carrying take-out container of water, as well. He forces Mrs. Pong to drink same.*)

MULLEIMER. Wasser, gnädige Frau. (*Yoko rushes into room. A teabag tag waves from her take-out container.*)

YOKO. Ochao dozo. (*Yoko kneels near Mrs. Pong and forces the old Chinese woman to drink tea. Each of them now pours liquid into the old Chinese woman, who squeals a lot, but seems nonetheless grateful. Each ad libs in his or her own language such phrases as "Drink up. You'll feel better, etc."*)

MULLEIMER. Trinken sie doch, meine Gute. Dann gehts ihnen gleich besser. Ja, ja. Ist schön gut. (*Wastba watches them a while before speaking.*)

LAPOUBELLE. (*Pointing to Yoko's contribution.*) Ca, c'est pas de l'eau, n'est-ce pas?

PATUMIERA. (*Also pointing to teabag.*) Dev' essere qualcosa Orientale.

MULLEIMER. (*Slamming Mrs. Pong's back.*) Fühlen Sie sich besser? Ja? (*Wastba now stands poised, her hand outstretched to greet them all.*)

WASTBA. Isn't that sweet of you all? Gifts for the Old Oriental! (*They all spin around and face her.*) Hi! (*She moves forward with overstated confidence and friendliness, pumping their hands in greeting.*) I'm your teacher. Debbie Wastba. (*Each rushes forward to deal with her outstretched hand. Patumiera will again grab LaPoubelle's hand before finding Wastba's. He will again use*

his tongue for emphasis, but this time will be shocked by Wasta's
reaction, which will be shock.)
MULLEIMER. Darf ich mich vorstellen, mein Name ist Fritz
Mülleimer.
WASTBA. Fritz? (*Laughs.*) Oh, the elevator . . . Yes.
MULLEIMER. Aber natürlich. Sie dürfen mich ruhig Fritz nennen.
WASTBA. Fritz?
MULLEIMER. Ja, Ja. Fritz. Ganz gewöhnlicher Deutscher Name.
Bin Deutscher, aber ursprünglich stammen wir aus Mesopotamien.
Während meine Vorfavern dort geblieben, so wäre ich jetzt Irake,
ha, ha. Zum Gluck waren sie Nomaden.
WASTBA. I haven't understood a single word of what you've said.
Do you know that?
MULLEIMER. (*Nonplussed. Chatty.*) Aber naturlich. Bin Deut-
scher, von Kopf . . . bis Fuss.
WASTBA. Look at that: bowing. Aren't you the polite one, now?
(*To LaPoubelle.*) You? What's your name, hmmm?
LAPOUBELLE. Enchanté, Madame.
WASTBA. First or last?
LAPOUBELLE. (*Bows; takes her hand and kisses it.*) Moi, je
m'appelle Jean-Michel LaPoubelle.
WASTBA. (*Giggles.*) Sheer poetry, I can tell you that.
PATUMIERA. (*It is here he executes his kiss.*) Io sono Carlo
Fredriko Rizzonini La Patumiera . . .
WASTBA. (*She recoils from him.*) Just watch it, you!! (*She
wipes her hand on her skirt. Yoko walks to the wastebasket and
picks it up.*)
YOKO. Watashi no namaewa Kuzukago Yoko desu.
WASTBA. Isn't that just simply one of the sweetest names you've
ever heard?
YOKO. (*Picks up wastebasket.*) Kuzukago Yoko. Kuzukago
Yoko.
PONG. (*Pointing to wastebasket.*) Ah, sē-lŏp-pŏng. Ngoi gwä lŏw
Pŏng thlee dūk-ä sē-lŏp-pŏng, wa.
WASTBA. (*Sees wastebasket.*) What's the matter with the waste-
basket? (*Pronounced as her name: WAH-STAH-BAH-SKET.
Yoko giggles. Puts wastebasket down. Giggles again.*) Okay, folks,
take your seats . . . (*Nobody moves. She talks louder.*) Take
. . . your . . . seats . . .
PATUMIERA. Take . . . you . . . zeets . . . (*Patumiera grabs*

his dictionary and starts looking for words. Smiling, he imitates Wastba, calling to ALL. No response will follow.)

WASTBA. No no no. Sit down. (She laughs nervously.) Doesn't anybody speak a little English? (They all continue to mill about her.) Sit down. (She laughs.) Watch me now. (She drags her chair out from behind her desk and sets it in the middle of the classroom. She slowly, carefully, demonstrates an act of sitting, first lifting out her skirts, then sitting, then folding her skirts demurely and then folding her hands into her lap. All stand around her in circle, watching and smiling.) See what I did? (Nobody responds, but Yoko, who giggles.) I sat. (All smile and nod. Wastba yells at them.) Sit down! (Nobody sits.) Stay calm, everybody. (She stands and walks the few steps to her desk. She turns away from the class. All watch, but for Patumiera, who is feverishly searching through his dictionary. Wastba turns to class again, smiling competently now.) Class, this could be one of the worst nights of our lives. (To LaPoubelle.) I want you to think seriously—deeply— about the following two words: sit down.

PATUMIERA. (Suddenly screams.) Eye!

WASTBA. What's the matter? Your eye? Soot?

PATUMIERA. (Struts happily to front of room, reading from his pad of paper.) Eye . . . have . . . eet! (Turns and picks up his chair over his head, displaying same to Wastba.) Eeet ees aye ki-eer.

WASTBA. Ki-air? Oh, no. No. It's chair! Chair. Good. It is a chair.

PATUMIERA. Alora, chair? Eeet ees a chair.

WASTBA. Good. Sit . . . in . . . it! (She stands and takes chair from Patumiera. She places chair on floor and bends Patumiera into it. She fails. He will not bend. All, but for Mrs. Pong, will soon assist Wastba.) Sit! Sit! (She motions to ALL to repeat word.) Sit! Sit!

MULLEIMER. Ach sitz! Komm sitz. (He begins to help push Patumiera into chair.)

ALL. (Repeat word.) Sit, Sitz, Seet! etc. (They all understand; push Patumiera downward.)

PATUMIERA. (He is panicked, as all are yelling at him. He stares at each with terror in his eyes.) Scusi. Non capisco.

YOKO. Seet! (She pushes his head from the top.)

27

WASTBA and OTHERS: Sit! Sit! Sit! (*Patumiera bends unwittingly and sits in chair, still confused.*)

WASTBA. (*Thrilled.*) Yes! He's sitting!

LAPOUBELLE. Seeting!

WASTBA. Right.

MULLEIMER. Zittsing!

WASTBA. Yes. (*To Patumiera.*) You're *sitting!* (*She applauds Patumiera. All applaud as well. Patumiera is no less panicked, but is smiling.*)

MULLEIMER. Zittsing!

WASTBA. (*To Mulleimer.*) Now you!

MULLEIMER. (*Sits with enormous grin of pride on face. He stretches legs way out in front of him, leans back, as though in a steam bath and "Zitzes."*) Zittsing!

WASTBA. Wonderful! (*To LaPoubelle.*) Now you!

LAPOUBELLE. Ah, oui. Mais, voila. Seeting. (*He sits.*)

PATUMIERA. Eet ees aye chair.

WASTBA. (*To Yoko.*) And you.

YOKO. Sitty. (*She sits.*)

WASTBA. (*Looks at Mrs. Pong.*) You did that on your own. Aren't you something? (*Patumiera tries to save face and crosses to his seat, pointing a finger to and lecturing old Mrs. Pong.*)

PATUMIERA. Eeet ees aye chair.

WASTBA. Now then. Hello. I'm Debbie Wastba. (*All are sitting, smiling now.*)

PATUMIERA. Scusi?

WASTBA. Huh?

MULLEIMER. Was?

YOKO. Nani?

MRS. PONG. Häaaaaa?

LAPOUBELLE. Comment?

WASTBA. (*From her desk.*) Listen, now, I'll just go really slow. (*Pauses; smiles.*) My name is Debbie Wastba. (*She writes her name on blackboard. Each takes notebook and copies down name.*) W-A-S-T-B-A. That's pronounced Wass-tah-bah: Wastba. (*She links each of the thre syllables together on board, in the following way: WA ST BA.*) Think of *Wah* as in wah-tah. Splash. Splash. *Stah* as in stah-bility. And *Bah* as in Bah-dum . . . as in (*Sings Dragnet theme.*) Bum-tah-bum-bum. Well, listen. It was literally double its length in its ancient, biblical form. (*Pauses.*) Actually, that tune was wrong. It would be much more like . . . (*Sings again, to tune of "My Funny Valentine."*) Bum bum-bum bum-bum-bum . . . bum bum-bum bum-bum-bum . . . bum bum-bum baaahhhmmmmmmm . . . (*Pauses: sees they are confused.*) Well, anyway, really, you can easily check your bibles if you want. (*Rummages through stack of papers on desk, holds up lesson plan.*)* This is our lesson plan. That's *lesson . . . plan*. Lesson plan. We're going to be together for several hours and I thought it would be highly professional and competent for me to make a plan. And I did. And here it is: (*She reads: smiling confidently.*) One. A pleasant welcome and normal chatter. For two, I've planned your basic salutations, such as the goods—good morning, good afternoon, good night, good luck and good grief. (*She laughs.*) That was a mildly amusing joke: "good grief." Later in the night—after we've learned a bit of English—you'll be able to, well, get the joke. (*Pauses.*) Let's move along. Three will be basic customs: ours here. (*Reading again.*) Four will be a short history of our English language. (*As the students take their notes, they, as we, begin to realize that Wastba is only writing the numbers 1–6 on to the blackboard—no words. They raise their hands in question, but she waves them away, barging ahead.*) Five will be the primary lesson of the primary English class, according to the book. And six will be the very essential verb "to be." At some point, we shall also inspect the very basic concept of silence. (*Smiles.*) Now then, as you can see, there are only six points to cover and hours and hours ahead in which to cover them. (*All stare blankly at her smiling face.*) Now then: Questions? (*Yoko sneezes.*) God bless you.

MULLEIMER. Gesundheit!

PATUMIERA. Salute!

LAPOUBELLE. À vos souhaits! (*Yoko sneezes again.*)

MULLEIMER. Nochmals. Gesundheit!

PATUMIERA. Salute, ancora.

LAPOUBELLE. À vos souhaits!

WASTBA. God bless you again! (*Laughs.*) That's a good one to learn. That's a basic custom, folks! (*Slowly: articulately.*) God bless you. Everybody. God bless you . . . (*All stare at her.*) God! . . . (*Waves arms above her head.*)

ALL. (*Repeating, while looking up.*) God . . .

*See addenda, end of play.

WASTBA. God bless . . . (*Touching her breasts on word "Bless."*)

ALL. God bless . . .

YOKO. God breast . . .

WASTBA. God bless *you!*

ALL. God bless *you!* (*All point to Wastba on word "you."*)

WASTBA. Thank you very much and I certainly hope he's paying attention, huh? (*Smiles to LaPoubelle. Points overhead to ceiling.*) Him. (*All raise their hands to ask a question.*)

YOKO. Shitsumon!

MULLEIMER. Duerfte ich Sie bitte etwas fragen! (*Wastba mubles "Let's see . . ." and pretends to be about to call on each of them, tantalizing them.*)

LAPOUBELLE. S'il vous plaît, mademoiselle . . . (*Wastba calls on LaPoubelle.*)

WASTBA. I . . . choose . . . *you!*

LAPOUBELLE. Ah, merci, mademoiselle! Qu'est-ce que vous avez dit? Je ne comprends pas . . . Moi, je pense que personne ne comprend . . . (*Smiles.*) Memê . . . enfin . . . meme moi. (*He smiles again.*) Compris?

WASTBA. Huh?

LAPOUBELLE. (*Looking about class.*) Y a-t-il quelqu'un qui parle français? (*All stare blankly at LaPoubelle.*)

WASTBA. I'm sorry, sir, but I don't speak . . . what you're speaking . . . French would be my first guess. Actually, that's quite obvious, right? (*Pauses; smiles.*) Right? (*No response.*) Parlez-vous français?

LAPOUBELLE. (*Instantly animated; speaks rapidly.*) Ou-ay! Français et seulement français! O la la! . . . je suis tellement heureux de vous entendre aussi parler français!

WASTBA. You're not French?

LAPOUBELLE. Comment?

WASTBA. Are you Swiss?

LAPOUBELLE. J'ai peur que je n'ai pas compris . . .

WASTBA. Don't the Swiss speak something like French?

LAPOUBELLE. Je ne comprends pas tout. Parlez plus lentement, s'il vous plait, chere mademoiselle . . .

WASTBA. Are you from Luxembourg?

LAPOUBELLE. Dîtes-le en français, s'il vous plaît.

WASTBA. It must be your accent . . .

LAPOUBELLE. *Comment?*

WASTBA. I'm a little anxious tonight . . .

LAPOUBELLE. Si vous le disiez en français, chère mademoiselle . . .

WASTBA. What?

LAPOUBELLE. Quoi?

WASTBA. Yes, thank you very much. (*To the class.*) Listen, which of you speaks a little English?

PATUMIERA. (*After a long pause: a short silence.*) Scusi?

WASTBA. Is that Greek?

PATUMIERA. Io . . . Non capisco . . .

WASTBA. Spanish, I'll bet.

PATUMIERA. Per piacere? Io . . .

WASTBA. (*She will tap out rhythm with her foot to Spanish words.*) I used to know a little Spanish . . . let's see . . . Me voy a lavar un poco para quitarme la arena que tengo pegada.

PATUMIERA. Scusi?

WASTBA. Don't you get it? It's beach talk. It means, "I'm going to wash the sand from my body." If some greaseball-type bothers you at the beach, that's what you say. My friend Ramon Vasoro taught me that. (*They all stare at her, blankly.*) Well, now, that's probably enough chatter. Do you have all your slips? (*No response.*) Slips? (*No response.*) Your slips. From the office. (*No response. She walks to LaPoubelle and begins rummaging through his briefcase.*) Excuse me.

LAPOUBELLE. Qu'est-ce que vous faites là? (*She continues to rummage.*) Pardoneez-moi, mademoiselle, mais qu'est-ce que vous voulez? (*She continues to rummage.*) Si vous m'expliquez ce que vous cherchez, j'essayerai de la trouver! (*No response.*) Mais, chère mademoiselle . . . Bordel! Quelle belle soirée!

WASTBA. (*She finds his slip.*) This! (*She waves it to class.*) Give me your slips. (*All smile and rummage about looking for their slips, which each finds and hands to Wastba. As she collects each slip, she reads each name, mispronouncing each.*) LaPoo . . . Is this a name?

LAPOUBELLE. LaPoubelle. Je m'appelle Jean Michel LaPoubelle. C'est cela? C'est mon nom que vous voudriez? C'est tout?

WASTBA. That's very unique. (*To Mulleimer.*) Where's yours? (*Takes slip, tries to read it.*) Is this of Slavic persuasion? (*Squints. She moves to Mrs. Pong and plucks the slip that has been stapled* to Pong's sleeve, not looking away from Mulleimer's slip.) Look at all these vowels. (Hands slip to Patumiera, who is staring into Yoko's blouse, not paying attention to Wastba. He takes the slip from her.) Can you pronounce this?

PATUMIERA. Grazie . . .

WASTBA. I don't think that's right. (Squints. Looks again.) Maybe. How's your eye? (Smiles at all.) I have new hard contacts. I hated the soft ones. Had to wash them every night. I went back to hard . . . (Blank stares all around.) Contacts. (Smiles.) Okay. There's a perfectly fine place to begin. (She will walk to Mulleimer and pluck his eyeglasses from his astonished face.)

MULLEIMER. Ah! (He is nearly blind without glasses and will soon feel his way, looking for Wastba.)

WASTBA. These are . . . (She reaches out. Plucks glasses.) . . . eyeglasses.

MULLEIMER. Meine Brille!! (He accidentally gropes Wastba, grabbing her breast in one absolutely clean move. All see and are amazed. Patumiera stands. He is vaguely ouraged.)

WASTBA. OH God!

PATUMIERA. EEEAYY!

WASTBA. (Shocked and amazed.) I'm going to try to overlook that . . . (Takes a deep breath.) God! Let's go on. (To all.) These are eyeglasses. It's a new word. Learn it. Eyeglasses. (Tries them on.) Oooooo. You must be blind as a bat. (Smiles again.) Eyeglasses. Eye-glasses. Eyeee-glasssezzzz . . . (Waves arms.) Everybody! Eyeee-glassezzz.

YOKO. Everiii—Eyeee-grasssezzz . . .

WASTBA. Good! Eyeee-glasssessssszzz . . . (Waves her arms.) Eyeeee-glassezzz . . .

LAPOUBELLE. Eye-glassée.

PATUMIERA. Eye-glasso.

WASTBA. Eye-glasses.

MRS. PONG. Eye . . . eye . . . gassieh.

WASTBA. (Taps her foot to lead her students' chant of the word "eyeglasses.") Everybody . . . eyeglasses . . . eyeglasses . . . etc. (Smiling, but clearly in panic.) Wonderful. Really. I wouldn't kid you. You're all just really wonderful. (She applauds her students, who are so pleased by her approval, they all scream the word "eyeglasses" at her again, each with his or her own indigenous accent.)

ALL. Eyee-glassy (zes) (o) (ée) etc. (*N.B. Mrs. Pong has been totally silent, but is awake, staring at all that goes on, smiling deeply, nibbling food.*)

WASTBA. Just really and sincerely terrific. Really. Terrific. Sincerely. (*Pauses.*) Oh God . . . (*Smiles.*) Now watch. (*She points to her eye.*) These are . . . contacts. (*No reply.*) Contacts. (*No reply. She touches eye.*) Contacts. (*Suddenly, she stiffens, blinking. A contact lens has popped out of her eye and fallen on to the floor.*) Oh . . . my . . . dear . . . God! (*They all stare dumbly as Wastba crawls around floor.*) Help me! It's on the floor!

LAPOUBELLE. Floor! (*He writes the word down. They look from one to the other, dumbly. Yoko and Patumiera move to her.*)

WASTBA. Help me! I'm not insured! (*Suddenly, she stops them from stepping on lens.*) Don't anybody move! (*They all look away from her. She falls back down on the floor.*) I got it! (*She wets the tip of her index finger, right hand, with which she stabs at lens. When it sticks to the tip of her finger, she screams.*) I really got it! Oh! Lucky break! (*She transfers lens to her mouth.*) Thank God, huh? (*She takes it out of mouth, holds it to light, looks at it, places it back into her mouth. She squints at class. She stands, smiling.*) I said, "Thank God, huh?" (*She looks at it, holding the lens toward the light, squinting. Mulleimer, blinded, has raised his hand, politely, but high in air. He holds his position.*) I'll have to go wash it off. (*She walks to door.*) I'll be right back. (*Wastba exits. There is silence in the room for a moment. Mulleimer breaks the silence, smiling to all.*)

MULLEIMER. Fräulein Lehrerin, hab ein kleines Problemchen! Bin ein bisschen schwer hörig. Gewöhlich bin ich ja Lippenleser, und das hilft schon, aber sie hat mir dock die Brille weggeschnappt, und jetzt kann ich nicht mehr sehen was ich nicht hören kann.

TRANSLATOR. Teacher, I've got a problem here. I'm a little hard of hearing, so usually I lip-read, which helps, but you took my glasses, so now I can't see what I don't hear. (*There is a moment of silence in the room, as all stare at spot where once there was a transparent contact lens. Patumiera is the first to break the silence. He seems angry with LaPoubelle.*)

PATUMIERA. (*To LaPoubelle.*) Che Gazzi ai detta?

TRANSLATOR. What the hell did you say to her?

YOKO. (*Very confidently, takes* c.) Kore wa akirakani totaru imashon no senjutsu desuyo.

TRANSLATOR. This is clearly a "total immersion" tactic.

PATUMIERA. Scusi?

YOKO. Konna hanashi o kiitakatoga arimasu. Otokono hito ga banana o te ni motte kyohitso ni haitee kitandesutte. Ban-ban to sakebinagara.

TRANSLATOR. I once heard of a man running into a classroom with a banana yelling "Bang-bang!" . . .

YOKO. Konna funi. (*Yoko runs out of classroom.*)

TRANSLATOR. Watch, I'll show you.

PATUMIERA. (*To LaPoubelle.*) Scusi? Che Gazzi ai detta?

TRANSLATOR. Now, what do you say to her?

YOKO. (*Runs back into classroom.*) Ban-ban. Tokyo deno dekigoto deshita. Amerikajin no bijinesuman no tame no nihongo no kurasu.

TRANSLATOR. It was in Tokyo. In a Japanese class for American businessmen.

YOKO. Kekkyoku Amerikajintachi wa sono hito o tatakinomeshite, motte ita banana o toriagechattan desutte.

TRANSLATOR. The way the story goes, the Americans beat the man up and took his banana.

PATUMIERA. Eh tu non vuoi rermare, eh?

TRANSLATOR. You're not going to stop, are you?

YOKO. Nani?

PATUMIERA. "Nani?" Se quella é inglese, tu' accenta è miserable . . . Un Orechio di stagno . . .

TRANSLATOR. "Nani?" If that's English, then your accent is intolerable. Language-wise, you've got a tin ear. (*Patumiera moves to Wastba's desk. Yoko begins copying down phrases from her phrasebook.*)

MULLEIMER. Entschuldigen Sie, Fraeulein Lehrerin, dürfte ich Sie bitte privat sprechen?

TRANSLATOR. Excuse me, teacher. May I have a private word with you?

LAPOUBELLE. Excusez-moi?

MULLEIMER. Fraeulein Lehrerin! Fraeulein Lehrerin!

TRANSLATOR. Teacher! Teacher!

PATUMIERA. (*To LaPoubelle.*) Ma, che hai fatto a lui adesso?

TRANSLATOR. Now, what did you do to him?

LAPOUBELLE. (*To Mulleimer.*) Que voulez-vous?

MULLEIMER. Entweder bringen Sie mir die Lehrerin oder lassen Sie mich in Ruhe, OK?

TRANSLATOR. Either get the teacher or get off my back, OK?

LAPOUBELLE. Une bonne classe, hein? Je suis très, très content. (*LaPoubelle has a small white paper bag filled with candies. He smiles and eats.*)

TRANSLATOR. Quite a class, huh? I'm very pleased by the way things are going.

MULLEIMER. Kann nicht behäupten, dass ich die Amerikaner verstehe. Warm und Freundlich sind sie ja, aber sie nehmen man die Brille weg, und warum, wenn ich Fragen darf, warum?

TRANSLATOR. I can't pretend to understand Americans. They're warm and friendly, but they take your eyeglasses and why, I ask you, why?

MULLEIMER. Und was mich so masslos aergert ist dass niemand von Euch Schweinehunden mir hilft!

TRANSLATOR. And why, I keep wondering, won't any of you sons of bitches help me get them back?

MULLEIMER. Falls ich Ihnen sage ein Baum stuerzt im Walde, und kein Mensch hier spricht ein Wort Deutsch, stuerzt dann der Baum, oder nicht?

TRANSLATOR. If I tell you a tree falls in the forest and nobody in here speaks any German, then does the tree ever fall? (*LaPoubelle offers candy to Mulleimer, placing piece on Mulleimer's desk. Mulleimer stares down blindly. Angrily, Mulleimer knocks the candy away.*)

LAPOUBELLE. Est-ce que vous vous rendez compte combien vous êtes impoli?

TRANSLATOR. Do you have any idea how rude you're being? (*LaPoubelle picks up candy and sits; sulks. Patumiera crosses to Yoko again; sits.*)

YOKO. (*Taking over class as though teacher.*) Ne. Minna kitte-kudasai. Hitotsu narai mashitayo. Eigo desuyo.

TRANSLATOR. Listen, everybody. I think I've learned something. I have some English here.

YOKO. (*In English, after checking her phrasebook and notes. Her accent is extremely heavy.*) I am starbing to . . . dess. (*She giggles.*)

TRANSLATOR. I am starving to death.

PATUMIERA. Si. Si, si. Si, si, si.

YOKO. (*In English; heavy accent.*) I would like my check, my rolls and my orangeee . . . (*Yoko teaches words to all.*)

MRS. PONG. Checoo . . .

PATUMIERA. Lolls . . .

YOKO. Lolls? Na. Rolls.

LAPOUBELLE. Orange.

YOKO. Watashiwa kotogakko de tomikakino seisekiga tottemo yokattandesuyo. Hontowa watashiwa kotobao umaku tsukaikonasemasu. (*Pauses; smiles at all.*)

TRANSLATOR. I got really good grades in high school for creative writing and public speaking. I've got a way with words.

YOKO. Watashino ie wa mukashikara benjutsu ni taketeite, sono rekishi wa mesopotamia made sakanoborundesu. (*She giggles at a blank-faced Patumiera.*)

TRANSLATOR. We have a history of oratory dating all the way back to Mesopotamia.

PATUMIERA. (*Frustrated by her incomprehensible language.*) Non ho capito nemmena una parole che tu hai detta, mia stuzzicadente. Ma perche tu sei cosi magra? Non piàce a mangiare o sei stanca di mangiare il riso?

TRANSLATOR. I haven't understood word one of what you've just babbled, toothpick. How come you're so skinny, huh? Don't you like food or do you just pick at your rice?

LAPOUBELLE. (*To Yoko.*) Je n'ai plus que douze heures et demie pour apprendre l'anglais, sinon je suis un homme mort. (*LaPoubelle grins as though his confession is totally unimportant.*)

TRANSLATOR. I've got 12 and ½ hours left in which to learn English or else I might as well be dead.

YOKO. Nani? (*Patumiera sees that LaPoubelle has moved in on Yoko. Sits on desk next to Yoko, squeezing LaPoubelle off desk completely. Yoko and Patumiera each take candy from LaPoubelle, which they dislike and discard.*)

LAPOUBELLE. Demain matin de bonne, j'ai un rendez-vous extrèmement important.

TRANSLATOR. I have an enormously important business meeting in the morning.

LAPOUBELLE. Si j'échoue, tout ma société d'assurance sera en faillite. Je perdrais mon job, ma jeune femme, mes enfants seraient obliges de quitter leur école privée . . . (*Yoko and Patumiera turn away from LaPoubelle.*)

TRANSLATOR. If I fail, my entire insurance company will bankrupt. Then I'll lose my job, my young wife and my children will have to drop out of private school . . . (*LaPoubelle stands at c., talking to no one in particular.*)

LAPOUBELLE. Je n'aurai plus qu'à me tuer.

TRANSLATOR. I'll have to kill myself. (*LaPoubelle sees that Yoko is no longer paying attention—is bored—and now smiling at Patumiera. LaPoubelle moves to Mrs. Pong, as she nods to him, seeing that he is trapped and alone at c.*)

MRS. PONG. Wa, wa.

LAPOUBELLE. (*To Mrs. Pong.*) Vous, vous ètes mariéé, veuve ou divorcée?

TRANSLATOR. Are you married, widowed or divorced?

PONG. M goi nay. Ngoi m hiěng gŏn nay mūn mwŭt wä. Nay gŏng mŏn-mŏn yä-ä yē. Ngoi ännäm gai wä.

LAPOUBELLE. Veuve! Je suis désolé. J'espère que la n'a pas trainé.

TRANSLATOR. I'm sorry to hear that. I hope it wasn't a lingering death.

PONG. Thlee mwŭt-ä : Yea thlee, toi mä siěk-ä?

TRANSLATOR. Give me a clue : animal? vegetable? or mineral?

LAPOUBELLE. Oui, ça va mieux comma ça. Moi mème, j'ai perdu ma première femme . . .

TRANSLATOR. That's a relief. I myself lost my first wife . . .

MRS. PONG. Toi?

TRANSLATOR. Vegetable? (*Pong has taken a piece of candy from LaPoubelle's bag during the above exchange.*)

LAPOUBELLE. Non, elle m'a quitté.

TRANSLATOR. No. She ran away.

LAPOUBELLE. Elle m'a laissé un petit mot me disant qu'elle s'ennuyait avec moi.

TRANSLATOR. She left a note saying I was boring.

PONG. Haa?.

LAPOUBELLE. Emmerdant, quoi.

TRANSLATOR. I said "boring."

PONG. Ahhhh.

LAPOUBELLE. Ma nouvelle femme est plutôt jeune. Elle aussi me trouve emmerdant.

TRANSLATOR. I have a young wife now. She finds me boring as well.

LAPOUBELLE. Heureusement, j'ai assez confiance en moi-même pourque ça ne m'ébranle pas.

TRANSLATOR. Luckily, I'm secure enough about my personality not to have to worry about such matters. (*Mrs. Pong throws her head back, snores loudly. Her head drops down to her chest. She is asleep, snoring loudly. She has, possibly, spat LaPoubelle's candy to floor. Patumiera and Yoko stare across to him. LaPoubelle is shocked and amazed and opens his suitcoat, trying to hide the sleeping Mrs. Pong from his classmates.*)

LAPOUBELLE. (*To Mulleimer.*) Elle est fatiquée, en plus elle est très vielle. Alors, je lui ai conseillé de se reposer.

TRANSLATOR. She's very old and is obviously exhausted. I've convinced her to get some rest.

MULLEIMER. Bitte keine ploetzlichen Bewegungen! Kann nur Schatten sehen. Es ist einfach schrecklich.

TRANSLATOR. Try not to make any sudden moves. I can only see shadows, and it's terrifying.

MULLEIMER. Wenn ich ganz still sitze und die Augen schliesse, ist es doch viel weniger beaengstigend.

TRANSLATOR. It's a lot less scary for me if I just sit here and close my eyes. (*Mulleimer does so, allowing his head to drop in sleeping position. Patumiera and Yoko stare at LaPoubelle, who stares at Mulleimer and Mrs. Pong, thinking he has put both of them to sleep. LaPoubelle sits; bows his head, silence.*)

PATUMIERA. Ho nostalgico, Io.

TRANSLATOR. I am homesick.

YOKO. Uchi ga koishiiwa.

TRANSLATOR. I am homesick.

PATUMIERA. (*Moving toward Wastba's desk.*) Ma fortunamento per noi abbiamo una buona maestra . . . simpatico, riguardosa, gentile . . . (*Patumiera touches Wastba's jacket on coat tree.*)

TRANSLATOR. Lucky for us we've got ourselves a great little teacher . . . warm . . . considerate . . . gentle . . . (*Suddenly we hear a bloodcurdling scream—Wastba's—from offstage, beyond the door, somewhere deep in a dark corridor. There is a moment of silence before each stands and comments.*)

MULLEIMER. Was war das? Unser kleiner kürbis vielleicht?

TRANSLATOR. What was that? Could that be our little pumpkin?

PATUMIERA. (*Also stands.*) La madonna sta in un imbroglio.

TRANSLATOR. Sounds like that madonna's in trouble!

LAPOUBELLE. Notre adorable artichaut! Mon dieu!

TRANSLATOR. Our darling little artichoke! My God!

YOKO. (*Standing.*) Sensei wa amerika de tatta hitorino watashino tomodachi nanoni.

TRANSLATOR. She's the only true friend I have in America! (*LaPoubelle moves quietly to the door. Suddenly, Wastba bursts into the room, slamming the door in LaPoubelle's face. He disappears from our view, squashed behind door, into wall. Wastba closes door now and presses her back against same. She holds Smietnik's mop in her hand.*)

LAPOUBELLE. Mademoiselle . . . (*He reaches for her and she screams, immediately handing mop to LaPoubelle, who places same behind coat tree, flat on floor, out of audience's view of same.*)

WASTBA. Yaaa-iiiiii!!! GJJ! (*LaPoubelle scoots back to his chair and sits. Wastba continues to lean heavily against door, keeping it closed. Wastba is incredibly frightened. She begins to speak. Her mouth moves, her lips form words, but there is no voice under them. Finally, the words are audible. All have been staring intently, wondering no doubt if this has all been part of an intensive study of primary English.*) There's . . . there's a . . . there's a very dirty man . . . (*Rubs her face; looks down first.*) There's a very dirty man out there . . . (*She giggles.*) In the ladies' room. (*She waits for response. There is none.*) There's a man in the ladies' room. (*Pauses.*) He . . . touched . . . (*Pauses; then speaks in determined way.*) He tried to hug me but, thank God, he was on his knees so he couldn't reach. (*Wipes brow.*) I wouldn't want to tell you what he did reach, however.

PATUMIERA. Che successo?

WASTBA. I said I wouldn't tell you! What are you, a tell-me-a-story freak or something??

PATUMIERA. Scusi?

WASTBA. Yuh. Sure.

MULLEIMER. Ich kann weder hören noch sehen. Könnte mir Bitte jemand helfen???

TRANSLATOR. I can't hear or see. Could somebody help me?

LAPOUBELLE. Mais calmez-vous. Vous êtes affreusement tendue.

MULLEIMER. Wer ist das?

WASTBA. (*Completely panicked.*) Oh . . . my . . . God . . .

(*Screams.*) *Tranquility!* (*Spins in circles.*) Got . . . to . . . get
. . . calm! (*Yells at class.*) Calm down!
MULLEIMER. (*Stands in front of Wastba.*) Wo ist meine Brille?
WASTBA. I know you're upset, but can you imagine how *I* feel?
(*She washes herself—her hands and arms—with "Wash-'n-Dri"
napkins from her sack.*) He . . . was . . . enormous. Eight or
nine feet tall!
MULLEIMER. Wo ist meine Brille, Fräulein?
WASTBA. For God's sake, this is no time for foreign language
problems! (*Pauses.*) He couldn't have been eight or nine feet tall.
I must be hysterical. Sit down. (*She sits, and they all sit, but for
Mulleimer.*) I'm sitting. Why don't you whistle something? (*She
whistles.*) I'm whistling. (*She pauses.*) I'm hysterical. Why don't
you change the subject? Class. I'm changing the subject— (*She
smiles.*) We must move on. Whatever is happening is happening in
the ladies' room and corridor and not in our room. (*Smiles, locks
door again, Mulleimer stands nearby.*) Our door is locked. Our
room is safe. (*Pauses.*) Things make sense here.
MULLEIMER. (*In front of Wastba, near door.*) Meine Brille?
Wo ist sie?
WASTBA. (*Pounds fist onto desk, loudly.*) Stop following me
around, damn it. I said things make sense in here and now I really
mean it!
MULLEIMER. (*Moves quickly, blindly, back to his desk. Students
assist him—lead him.*) Wie bitte?
WASTBA. We're going to just have to continue our class in a
sane and orderly fashion. Otherwise, we perish. (*To Mulleimer.*)
You want to perish?
MULLEIMER. Wie bitte?
WASTBA. Sit down.
LAPOUBELLE. Zeet! Zeet! (*Mulleimer finds his way back to his
chair and sits.*)
WASTBA. (*To LaPoubelle.*) You! You want to perish?
LAPOUBELLE. (*Stands; recites the word, tentatively.*) Per . . .
per- . . . per-ashh . . .
WASTBA. "Ish," not "ash." There's a good word to learn. Perish.
(*Writes "Perish" on blackboard.*)
PATUMIERA. Mia cara signorina . . .
WASTBA. (*Turns to him; angrily.*) Sit down and learn the word
"perish." (*Pauses. Patumiera stops, turns, rushes to his seat, sits.*)

I'm getting calm. If you were smart, you'd go for calm, too. See?
If I were any calmer, I'd be boring.
LAPOUBELLE. Ma chere mademoiselle, il y a encore un petit
probleme . . . *encore* . . .
WASTBA. I said "Boring."
YOKO. (*Stands suddenly; takes over. Points to her head in gesture
of "J understand now."*) Ah! Bowling. (*She mimes bowling.*)
MULLEIMER. Wo ist meine Brille?
WASTBA. I don't understand a word you're saying!
MULLEIMER. Ich verstehe kein Wort von dem was
sie sagen.
LAPOUBELLE. Je ne comprends pas un mot de ce
qu'ils disent.
PATUMIERA. Non capisco una parola di quel che
dicono.
YOKO. Watashiwa ka rerano hanashiteru kotoga
wakarimasen.

(*All at
same
time
twice.*)

WASTBA. (*Writes the word "English" beside the word "Perish"
on the blackboard. Yells; stopping their words.*) I'm afraid you're
going to have to just get it through your heads that this is an
English class and the language I'm afraid I must *insist* we all speak
is . . . for the love of God . . . English. (*She points to the
words.*) Attention must be paid to these words: they both end in
"i-s-h." (*Pauses.*) Let's hear them. (*No response. Waves her
arms.*) English. Perish. (*No response.*) English. Perish. English.
Perish. I *demand* you follow! (*She points at Patumiera.*) You!
English. Perish. (*Patumiera is again in panic. He smiles and
shrugs and tries to repeat what she has said: tries to please her.*)
PATUMIERA. (*Mimicking.*) English. Perish.
WASTBA. Very good. (*Waves arms.*) Everybody now: Hit it!
(*Screams.*) English! Perish.
LAPOUBELLE. English. Per-EESH.
WASTBA. English! Perish!
ALL. (*Each yells the words "English! Perish!" in an accent indige-
nous to his or her own particular country.*) Iingliish! Glishie!
Anglish! (Etc.) (*Mulleimer leans forward trying to whisper in the
direction of Wastba's voice, but instead whispers in the clear.*)
MULLEIMER. Fräulein! . . .
WASTBA. (*To all.*) That was wonderful! See? You can get it if

41

you really want . . . But you must try . . . Just like the song says . . .

MULLEIMER. (*Whispers again.*) *Fräulein!*

WASTBA. Huh?

MULLEIMER. (*Whispers again; embarrassed to be without his glasses. Tries to appear as though all in his life is normal.*) *Fräulein!*

WASTBA. (*Whispers across to him.*) *What do you want?*

MULLEIMER. (*Whispers.*) *Wo ist meine Brille, Fräulein?*

TRANSLATOR. (*Whispers.*) *Where are my glasses, lady?*

WASTBA. (*Whispers.*) *Huh?*

MULLEIMER. *Wo ist meine Brille, Fräulein?*

WASTBA. (*Whispers.*) You will either get a goddamn English word out of that mouth of yours or just drop all talk! . . . (*Pauses; she still whispers.*)

MULLEIMER. (*Whispers.*) *Verstehen Sie denn nicht dass ich nicht verstehe?*

TRANSLATOR. (*Whispers.*) *Don't you understand that I don't understand?*

WASTBA. (*Whispers.*) *Don't you understand that I don't understand?* (*Mrs. Pong stands and begins to walk to the closed door. She is holding her stomach and seems to be experiencing pain. She bows to Wastba, who seems astonished to see the old woman's move to door. To old Mrs. Pong.*) What are you doing? (*Mrs. Pong bows to LaPoubelle and Patumiera, who stand and return her bow.*)

LAPOUBELLE. Bon soir, madame.

PATUMIERA. Bonn sera . . .

WASTBA. Where are you going? (*Mrs. Pong bows.*) Where do you want to go to do what? (*Mrs. Pong bows again.*) Don't open that door! (*Wastba leaps between Mrs. Pong and the door.*) Didn't you hear me? (*Wastba shoves Mrs. Pong back away from door and knocks her down. Mrs. Pong squeals. All go to Pong and help her up.*)

LAPOUBELLE. Elle lui fait mal!

TRANSLATOR. She hurt her!

PATUMIERA. Le ho fatto male!

TRANSLATOR. She hurt her!

YOKO. Sensei wa ranbo o shimashita!

TRANSLATOR. She hurt her!

WASTBA. I'm sorry. I didn't mean to shove that hard. Push always grows to shove, I swear to God!

LAPOUBELLE. Nom de Dieu, vous avez vu ca? Elle a frappé cette vieille vietnamienne.

WASTBA. I didn't mean to push this old Chinese lady around . . . or certainly down! (*Looks at all, who are each staring amazed at Wastba.*)

YOKO. (*Yells, as will all that follow.*) Dou shitanodesuka?

PATUMIERA. Che è successo?

LAPOUBELLE. Qu'est-ce qui se passe?

MULLEIMER. Ich flehe Sie an meine Brille!

WASTBA. What the hell is happening in here anyway? (*Mrs. Pong makes another run at the door, more confirmed this time. She succeeds in reaching the knob this time. Wastba whacks at her hand on the knob.*) Hey! (*Wastba pulls Mrs. Pong away from the door.*) I told you once, damn it! Now get away from this door! (*Wastba drags Mrs. Pong back to her desk and seats her.*) Now, damn it! I've told you there's a dirty man out there. (*She holds Mrs. Pong by the back of her jacket.*) At your age, what the hell are you looking for, anyway? (*Mrs. Pong whimpers, pulling back. All are shocked, staring.*) You could get hurt out there! (*Holding Mrs. Pong still by back of her jacket.*) Try to understand . . .

MRS. PONG. (*She breaks free and runs to her desk, screaming.*) Ahhh-yiiiii . . .

WASTBA. Why are you screaming?

MRS. PONG. Ahhhh-yiiii!

WASTBA. Stop it!

MRS. PONG. Ooooo. (*She sits; whimpers. She eats.*)

WASTBA. (*Leaning over Mrs. Pong.*) Did I hurt you, old Chinese woman?

MRS. PONG. (*Moving backwards as a crab.*) Ahhh-yiiiiii-ahhhh . . .

YOKO. Kio ochitsukete! Kitto nani ka riyu ga arundesuwa.

WASTBA. (*To class.*) I don't even know her name. (*To Yoko.*) What's her name? (*No response.*) Aren't you family? (*No response. Wastba grabs large red tag from around Mrs. Pong's neck.*) There's a tag on her neck . . . (*Reads.*) "Hi. My name is Zink?" (*Strains to read.*) I can't read this! . . . (*To Mrs. Pong.*) What's your name? (*No reply.*) Don't you even know

your own name? (*Reads tag again.*) "I don't speak English . . . "
(*To all.*) Oh, no need to be modest. (*Pats Mrs. Pong, who
moans.*) "Mrs. Pong . . . " Is that your name: Mrs. Pong?
MULLEIMER. Meine Brille . . .
WASTBA. (*In panic; to Mulleimer.*) Hey, I've seen a lot worse
on laundries and restaurants . . . Wing, Ling, Ding . . . (*Shrugs.*)
But, listen. Pong's no picnic either, I guess . . . (*Wastba absently
pats Pong's head, unintentionally scaring the old lady again.*)
MRS. PONG. Yiiii—iiii . . .
WASTBA. (*To Mrs. Pong; leaning in to her.*) Don't you under-
stand anything? (*No response.*) What I did I did for your own
good . . . (*N.B.: Throughout above, Wastba has been holding
Mrs. Pong erect in her chair.*)
LAPOUBELLE. Je pense que vous devriez vraiment vous expliquer.
Après tout, vous l'avez poussé parterre.
WASTBA. Everybody here is my witness, right?
PATUMIERA. Ho bisogno di un splegazione, adesso.
WASTBA. I know you're all upset. I'm upset too . . . (*Mrs.
Pong whimpers.*) Now you're upset too . . . (*Wastba smiles at
all.*) We're just going to have to drop our mutual differences for a
while and learn some English. A common goal is always for the
common good . . .
LAPOUBELLE. Chère mademoiselle . . . Personne ne comprend
encore! Compris? Personne!
WASTBA. I said "common goal for common good." Don't you
ever pay attention? (*Wastba releases her hold on Mrs. Pong and
begins to move to the blackboard.*) These distractions will have to
stop. (*She picks up apple that Yoko brought to class for her.
Wastba smashes apple on desk. Yoko screams.*) One rotten apple
spoils a bunch. (*Wastba throws apple into wastebasket.*) One must
resist temptation. Mrs. Pong has managed to distract us . . .
She has, in short, managed to become our mutual rotten apple,
but . . . I needn't remind you that the object of this class is
clearly English and hardly some old Pong. (*Mrs. Pong sings "I
can't give you anything but love, baby" very quietly; a hum.
Reading from sheet at same time all babble questions about Mrs.
Pong and Wastba's wrestling match.*) . . . so if you'll kindly
and politely pay a little attention here, I'm going to give you the
history of English. (*Pauses; smiles.*) I picked this sheet up in the
office . . . early this morning. (*Wastba has now written the
words "The Great Vowel Shift" on the blackboard. Pong tries to

44

calm herself down by singing more loudly now. The words are sometimes clear. "Baby" is sung in English.)

MRS. PONG. *(To the tune of "J Can't Give You Anything But Love.")*

Bah, bah, bah, bah, bah, bah, bah, bah, bahhh . . . Ba-bee
Bah, bah, bah, bah, bah, bah, bah, bah, bahhh . . . Ba-bee.

WASTBA. "The Great Vowel Shift." *(Reading.)* "Compared to Old English, in phonological terms, Middle English's ĕ, ē . . . ī" . . . *(She writes the letters on blackboard as she lectures.)*

YOKO. IIII . . .

PATUMIERA. Eeee . . .

WASTBA. Ī, ē, ū . . .

LAPOUBELLE. Ooooo . . .

WASTBA. Please just quietly take notes, okay. "ō and ē . . . "

MRS. PONG. *(Jll and faint.)* Aaaaayyyyiiii . . .

WASTBA. Oh. *(Without looking up, continues reading.)* " . . . and ā were raised in their articulation. Middle English's ā, which comes from Old English's short ă, in open syllables, was fronted as well." *(Looks up at class.)* While this may see to mean little to you, it means even less to me, and I was born speaking English perfectly! *(Reads again.)* "The highest two Middle English front and back vowels, ī . . . "

YOKO. īiii

WASTBA. "and ū respectively, became sounds traditionally known as dipthongs . . . "

MRS. PONG. *(Collapses in unconsciousness, her head crashing down forward on her desk.)* Oooooo . . .

WASTBA. *(Continuing.)* "These changes in the quality of the long or tense vowels constitute what is known as . . . " *(Underlining each word as she says it.)* " . . . The Great Vowel Shift."

LAPOUBELLE. *(To Yoko.)* Mon Dieu. Mais la vieille vietnamienne! Elle est tombée dans les pommes.

PATUMIERA. Forse è la vechiai. Mi sembra che questa vechia ha due centi anni.

YOKO. Toshi no seikamo shiremasenne. Nihyakusai gurai ni mierudesho.

MULLEIMER. *(Head down, sulking.)* Wo ist meine brille? *(All gather around Mrs. Pong, rubbing her hands and ad libbing encouraging remarks.)*

YOKO. Shimpai shinakutemo daijobu desuyo.

45

LAPOUBELLE. Je vends les assurance de vie, et j'en ai vu de pires, croyez-moi!

PATUMIERA. Non fa paura, signora. Questa è una rechia. Ha bisogna di una riposa per un settimana e motto di medicazione. Conosca un dottore?

YOKO. Oisha san o shitte imasuka?

PATUMIERA. Conosca un dottore?

WASTBA. *(She now turns and faces them. For the first time in this sequence, she is aware that no one is paying any attention at all. She is furious. She throws the blackboard eraser and hits LaPoubelle's back. They all look up at her a bit frightened. Mrs. Pong as well. Patumiera picks up eraser from floor. Silence.)* Supposing I were to spring a little pop quiz right now, huh? Huh huh? Huh huh huh? Which one of you would even pass? *(She points to Patumiera.)* You? Could you pass?

PATUMIERA. *(He has eraser and whacks himself on head with same for emphasis. Chalk dust flies.)* Ho un dolore di testa.

LAPOUBELLE. Que j'ai mal a la tête.

MULLEIMER. Mir zerspringt der kopf.

YOKO. Atama ga itai wa.

MRS. PONG. Aaaii, Ngoi gä hai tiĕk wah.

WASTBA. Okay, I'm now preparing the quiz . . . *(Turns to board, grabs forehead.)* . . . You over there, you're giving me a headache. *(Looks at Patumiera. Patumiera smiles and then coughs.)*

PATUMIERA. *(To Wastba.)* Ho una brutta tosse. *(Holds his chest.)* Ho un dolore qui.

WASTBA. *(Turns and faces him, slowly.)* Can I believe my ears? It sounds like an unwanted tongue . . .

PATUMIERA. *(Holds his stomach, in pain.)* Ho un dolore di stomaco . . . *(Holds his thighs.)* Mi fanno male le gambe . . . *(Grabs his back, suddenly.)* Mi fa male le schiene!

WASTBA. And now lewd gestures, too!

PATUMIERA. Mi fa male il bracchio. Mi fa male l'orecchio. Ho i brividi. Ho febbre.

WASTBA. That does it, wop! I'm giving you a pop quiz!

PATUMIERA. Da ieri.

WASTBA. Take your pen and a piece of yellow lined paper and explain the Great Vowel Shift. Ten mintues, no open books.

PATUMIERA. *(Paying no attention.)* Da ieri.

WASTBA. *(Screams.)* *Are you taking this quiz or what?*

PATUMIERA. (*Humiliated to be yelled at in front of the others, he screams as well.*) Non capisco un cavalo di quel che dici! (*LaPoubelle is still standing near Mrs. Pong. He misunderstands the tension in the room, completely.*)

LAPOUBELLE. (*In French.*) On dirait qu'elle vit encore mais à peine. Et ce n'est pas grâce à vous . . . Quelle belle soirèe!

PATUMIERA. *Non capisco un cavolo do quel che dici!* (*Screaming at LaPoubelle.*) Che cavolo dicono?

LAPOUBELLE. (*Screams back at Patumiera.*) Qu'est-ce que vous dites, tireur de spaghetti? Hein? Sale macaroni? (*To the world.*) Ben, merde, alors! Quelle belle soirée! (*All continue their complaints, as Mulleimer chimes in as well.*)

MULLEIMER. *Himmel! Herr Gott! Donnerwetternocheinmar! Ich will meine Brille???*

WASTBA. What the hell do you want?

MULLEIMER. (*Groping his way toward the sound of Wastba's voice, his hand finds one of her breasts.*) Meine Brille! (*Wastba pulls back violently.*)

WASTBA. Oh . . . my . . . God!

MULLEIMER. (*Reaches toward her again.*) Meine Brille, Fräulein!

WASTBA. Goddammit, just keep your filthy little Dutch hands to yourself! Don't you think I've had enough sex for one night!

LAPOUBELLE. Sexe? (*Mulleimer reaches out toward her again and she slaps his face.*)

WASTBA. I can't believe it! You're trying it again! (*Silence in room as all stare amazed.*)

MULLEIMER. (*Shocked and amazed; still blind without his eyeglasses. He staggers back.*) Fraulein!

WASTBA. I'm sorry to have had to do that in front of everybody, but you did what you did in front of everybody. (*Mulleimer is not to be stopped now. He moves to Wastba once more, reaches for her one final time.*)

MULLEIMER. *Wo ist meine Brille?* (*He reaches out, she slaps.*)

WASTBA. Now that is the goddamned limit! (*She slaps Mulleimer again.*)

MULLEIMER. Arghhh!

WASTBA. I've told you five or six times, Dutchie! This is the twentieth century, ya' know! I don't have to take that kind of crap from anybody anymore.

MULLEIMER. Was ist denn? Wo bin ich?
PATUMIERA. Che sta succedendo? (*N.B.: Throughout the entire
section, Mrs. Pong has been watching, wide-eyed. Mrs. Pong will
soon make a break for the door again and will not, this time, be
stopped. Her moves will be enormous in that she will leap from
the floor, high into the air, several times, as she screams at Wastba
in rage. Mulleimer has bowed his head now in shame and humiliation and LaPoubelle is leading him back to his chair.*)
WASTBA. If you ever . . . ever! . . . take such a horrid liberty
again, I swear I will seek revenge . . . (*Pulls back; straightens
herself.*)
MULLEIMER. (*Whispered.*) Fräulein? . . .
WASTBA. If you're getting my message! (*No response. She waits
for an answer as she seats Mulleimer. Mrs. Pong begins her major
move now. She leaps up, screams, and threatens to karate chop
Wastba.*)
MRS. PONG. Eeiieewwwaamaaiiaaa!!!
WASTBA. Hey!
MRS. PONG. Nay kay kŭng wah! Nay kay kŭng mä ngoi dē
jŏm lŏn-nä nay lieng-gä siew äng nay gä gieng wah!
TRANSLATOR'S VOICE. Stay back! Stay back or I'll break both
of your arms and your neck too!
MRS. PONG. How-lä. (*Stands straight now. Leans back and nods
to Wastba, who stands by the door, staring, astonished.*) Ngoi chŭt
coi gä mwŭn wah. (*Mrs. Pong moves closer to Wastba and points
to Mulleimer, Patumiera, Yoko and LaPoubelle, one at a time,
angrily they try to calm Mrs. Pong down.*) Coi thlŏm gä gŏm ngoi
ngĭm thlŏm boy sui äng cui dē gom ngoy ngim yit boy chä äng
coi sē ngoi dē chut coi gä mwun hun thlee swa wah, how mah?
TRANSLATOR'S VOICE. I'm going out that door right now.
Those three made me drink three glasses of water and she made
me drink a cup of tea and now I'm going out the door and to the
bathroom, okay?
MRS. PONG. Na hiew ngoi gŏng mah, häää?
TRANSLATOR'S VOICE. Do you understand me?
MRS. PONG. (*Waves the terrified Wastba away from the door
and moves to it; stops, turns around, faces into room and yells at
Wastba.*) Ngoy sä-lä ngoy m sät gŏng fŏn wa, lë, hĩ ngoy sät gŏng
fŏn wah, ngoi dē m loy coi yä! Nay hiew ngoi gŏng mä?! Hä?!
TRANSLATOR'S VOICE. I'm sorry I don't speak English, but, if
I did speak English, I wouldn't be here! *Don't you understand*

that?! Okay?! (Making a final attempt to save Mrs. Pong, Wastba leans in and pleads with her, as all surround Mrs. Pong.)

WASTBA. Old Chinese woman, hear me. Don't go out there. I beg you . . .

MRS. PONG. *(She chases LaPoubelle, screaming.)* Ngoi coi lŏw yiek mieng gŏn gwä nä cŏw thlay hŏn-nieh wä! A sui gŏw näy cow-a, niek mä? Hä, hä-hä, hä-hä-hä?? *(In English to LaPoubelle.)* Sit! *(LaPoubelle hides behind chair.)*

WASTBA. My knee is bent to you. That's a beg. Please, Pong. Pong. Pong. I'm pleading, Pong. Back up to your student desk. Just throw it in reverse and back up. Please, Pong.

MRS. PONG. Nay hong huey lä-a. Ngoy chūt de chūt lë.

WASTBA. *(Moves to Mrs. Pong.)* I'll have to forceably detain you. I know it must rub your religion the wrong way, but what the hell choice are you offering me, huh? *(Wastba reaches for old Mrs. Pong's sleeve.)*

MRS. PONG. *(Raises her hand to chop. She screams.)* Nay kay kung! *(Wastba leans silently against blackboard now; head bowed.)* Ngoy loy fŏn thlay ga fŏn jüng yä . . . *(Mrs. Pong holds up four fingers.)*

TRANSLATOR'S VOICE. I'll be back in four minutes . . . *(Mrs. Pong waves her four fingers.)*

MRS. PONG. Thlay. Gä-wä.

TRANSLATOR'S VOICE. Four. Only. *(Repeating Chinese word and waving. She thinks Mrs. Pong has said goodby.)* Thlay, Pong, thlay Gä-wä . . .

ALL. *(Waving.)* Thlay, Gä-wä. *(Mrs. Pong stops, looks at Wastba, shrugs, bows, opens door and exits. As soon as Mrs. Pong has negotiated her exit, Wastba slams door closed tightly by hurling herself against same. There is silence in the room.)*

WASTBA. Well, listen . . . *(Smiles)* . . . maybe an old Oriental of her years just isn't cut out for a stiff class like ours . . . *(Walks to Mrs. Pong's desk, finds her slip and walks back to wastebasket, where she throws slip away, after tearing it to bits. She moves to desk. She sits. Folds her hands, smiles.)* Let's hope old Mrs. Pong finds another class . . . something more to her . . . well . . . fancy. *(Pause.)* Here we are again; just us. *(Pauses; smiles.)* Any questions?

PATUMIERA. Non ho capito nemmena una parola che tu hai detta!

49

TRANSLATOR. I haven't understood even one word of what you've said!

MULLEIMER. (*With overstated calm.*) Okay . . . (*Smiles a big smile.*) . . . Jetzt sitze ich und bin ruhiger . . .

TRANSLATOR. Okay . . . I'm sitting now and I'm calmer . . .

MULLEIMER. . . . also, wo ist meine Brille? (*He is now, as if to prove calmness, smiling rather idiotically.*)

TRANSLATOR. Now, where are my glasses?

WASTBA. (*Calling back.*) I'm not answering a single question until you're asking in English . . . (*Pauses.*) Sorry . . .

MULLEIMER. Wo ist meine Brille?

WASTBA. Nope.

MULLEIMER. (*Through clenched teeth.*) Wo ist meine Brille?

WASTBA. Uh uh . . .

MULLEIMER. Wo ist meine Brille? (*No response, as Wastba crosses her arms on her chest and shakes her head. Mulleimer stands now and screams.*) In Ordnung! Dann eben nicht! Dann bin ich eben blind! (*Mulleimer throws a tremendous temper tantrum. He screams. He throws his books. He breaks pencils and throws them onto the floor. He punches his desk. He beats the floor. Finally he sulks. Silence, as all stare in disbelief.*)

WASTBA. Why did you do that?

LAPOUBELLE. De tuote ma vie, je n'ai jamais vu une scene comme ça, jamais. Ça alors!

TRANSLATOR'S VOICE. In my entire life, I've never ever seen a scene like that! Wow!

PATUMIERA. Credi che abbia imparato qualcosa?

TRANSLATOR. Do you think he learned anything?

YOKO. (*She smiles and whispers to Patumiera.*) Eigo wa omotta-yorimo taihendesune . . .

TRANSLATOR. English looks a lot tougher than I thought . . . (*A soft knocking sound at door. All look up. Wastba squeals in terror. Silence, as all look from Wastba to door. Knocking resumes, as slow fade to black. Curtain.*)

END OF ACT ONE

N.B. Intermission is optional. If played *without* intermission, cut soft knocking at door from above.

I.H.

50

ACT II

Lights up on scene as it was, Wastba at blackboard. She writes* the word "Silence" on blackboard. All stare at her. She stares back at them. There is silence.

WASTBA. Silence. Can you hear it? (*Pauses; finger to word on blackboard.*) Silence.
LAPOUBELLE. Zi-lence?
WASTBA. Silence. That's what's wanted here: silence. Okay?
LAPOUBELLE. Ah, oui. C'est le même mot en francais: *silence.* (*Above* "silence" *in French.*)
WASTBA. Si-lonce. Right. Now let's hear you say the word in English: silence . . .
LAPOUBELLE. Oui, je comprends. (*Now in English.*) Silence.
WASTBA. (*Smiles.*) Perfect.
LAPOUBELLE. (*Puts his fingers to his lips and repeats word.*) Silence.
PATUMIERA. Silenco!
LAPOUBELLE. (*Looks sternly at Patumiera.*) Shhh.
WASTBA. Silence.
PATUMIERA. Zi-*lence?*
LAPOUBELLE. Shhhh.
WASTBA. Silence.
YOKO. Silence? (*Giggles.*)
LAPOUBELLE. Shhhh.
YOKO *and* PATUMIERA. Silence!
LAPOUBELLE. (*Angrily.*) Shhh!
WASTBA. (*Smiling to Patumiera and Yoko.*) That's much better . . . Silence.
YOKO *and* PATUMIERA. (*Happily.*) Silence! Silence!
LAPOUBELLE. (*Angrily, to both. In French again. He stands.*) Shhhh! Ecoutez! Silence, hein?
WASTBA. (*To LaPoubelle: angrily.*) Will you stop interrupting us?

*If intermission is taken, word "silence" should be already written on board. Also sense some time has passed wanted.

LAPOUBELLE. Mais, mademoiselle . . .

WASTBA. (*Placing her finger to her lips.*) Shhh.

LAPOUBELLE. (*Angrily.*) Bon. (*He sits. He is silent a moment.*)

YOKO and PATUMIERA. (*In unison. Pointing to LaPoubelle, they begin laughing.*) Silence. (*Yoko giggles.*)

WASTBA. (*Moves to her desk, sits on it and Mulleimer's glasses.*) Now then . . . Ohhh! (*Finds glasses.*) Look! I almost forgot! Not broken. Not broken. Didn't break them. (*She turns to Mulleimer.*) Your glasses . . . (*She puts them on his face.*) Here you go. (*Mulleimer is shocked and amazed and thrilled.*)

MULLEIMER. Meine Brille! (*He stands and looks at Wastba and at class, overjoyed.*) Ahhhh! Meine Brille! Ssank you.

WASTBA. (*Thrilled.*) Ahhh!

MULLEIMER. Ssank you . . . veriii mich . . .

WASTBA. (*Pointing to his mouth.*) English!

YOKO. Ahhh!

PATUMIERA. Ahhh!

MULLEIMER. Veri mich, yah!

WASTBA. (*Pointing to his lips.*) English, class! English! Immersion is working! (*She applauds Mulleimer, who bows.*) Bless you, Mr. Mancini . . .

MULLEIMER. (*Laughing and bowing.*) Veri mich, yahhh! (*The rest of the class now applauds, wildly laughing. They are extremely happy to be succeeding. They are now applauding and cheering. Wastba turns to them, delighted. She bows. Wastba laughs anxiously; bows.*)

WASTBA. Oh, my goodness. You're all expressing such approval! (*Mulleimer stands and bows as well.*) Oh, look at you! Excited . . . bowing, too . . . (*Wastba straightens up.*) Okay, now, let's settle. Settle, now, settle. (*Wastba is laughing quite happily. She searches through her satchels of books. She smiles to the class.*) I want you all to understand that while I have nothing . . . personally . . . against your tongues, I must teach this primary English class absolutely by . . . the . . . book. (*Smiles.*) I'm sure you understand. (*Pauses.*) Where's the book? (*Searches feverishly; finds book.*) I got it! (*Looks up, smiling. Produces small book covered in orange fabric, which she waves at class.*) I had to put ten dollars down on this. (*Smiles.*) A deposit.

(*Pauses.*) In this country, it's assumed you're going to lose . . . something. Nor do I. Not at ten dollars a shot. (*Smiles.*)

LAPOUBELLE. (*Recognizes a word and smiles as well.*) Sum-zing!

WASTBA. Hmmm.

LAPOUBELLE. Je comprends un peu. Sum-zing, par example: c'est quelquechose, n'est-ce pas?

WASTBA. *Will you please and kindly pay some attention! Sit down!*

LAPOUBELLE. (*Humiliated.*) Enfin, merde! C'est quelquechose! Ce n'est pas compliquè! (*They all sit.*)

ALL. Seetz . . . Sit dunn . . . Teetz . . . etc.

WASTBA. This is the book. Say it. Book. Book. Book.

ALL. Book. Book. Book.

WASTBA. (*Reads to them, clearly.*) "The object of the primary English class will be to teach the negative form." (*To the class.*) The negative should be right up your alleys. (*Reading again.*) "You will reach the negative through the positive . . . " (*To the class.*) Pay attention. (*Reads again.*) "You will reach the negative through the positive . . . " Okay . . . (*Reading.*) "Touch the floor and announce to class 'I can touch the floor.' " (*Pauses.*) Once again, I learn to lower myself in the name of higher learning. (*She drops to the floor.*) Okay. Here I am. Listen. (*She touches the floor and announces to class.*) I can touch the floor. (*Reads again from book.*) "Have they all said 'I can touch the floor!'?" (*Looks up.*) Has *who* all said "I can touch the floor!?" This is just tawdry . . . If they think I'm going to make a life of this, they're barking up the wrong tree . . . (*LaPoubelle suddenly drops out of his chair onto the floor, on all fours, as might a hound.*)

LAPOUBELLE. Flo-er! Flo-er! (*He moves toward Wastba grinning and yelping.*) Flo-er! Flo-er!

WASTBA. What is it?

LAPOUBELLE. Flo-er! Flo-er! (*He moves closer to her, even more houndlike. She pulls away, frightened.*)

WASTBA. What the hell are you doing? Get away from me! Sit! Scat! Heel! (*Screams.*) *Sit!!!*

MULLEIMER. (*Sits on the floor, touching it with two hands.*) Zeet? Zeet, fluur!

YOKO. (*Same.*) Flory.

PATUMIERA. (*Same.*) Scusi?

WASTBA. The floor! You're touching the floor! (*Demonstrates.*)

PATUMIERA. (*Shocked and amazed and thrilled; on his knees.*) Fleeer!

WASTBA. (*Flailing her arms about for them to follow.*) I can touch the floor! I can touch the floor. I can touch the floor!

ALL. I can touch the floor! (*In unison, in their varying accents.*)

WASTBA. (*Reading.*) "If they can touch the floor and have said so, show them how to touch the desk." (*Looking up.*) Okay, you sneaky devils, I can touch the desk.

LAPOUBELLE. Comment?

WASTBA. (*She runs to her desk; slaps same.*) I can touch the desk!

LAPOUBELLE. (*Walks to her desk.*) "I can tooooch le dest!"

WASTBA. (*Flailing her arms.*) Everybody! (*Screaming and whacking the desk.*) I CAN TOUCH THE DESK!

ALL. (*Screaming and whacking the desk as well.*) I . . . Toooch . . . Desttie. (*Etc.*)

WASTBA. (*Reads from book.*) "Simple parts of the body." What's simple, these days? (*She dances and slaps her feet.*) Feet! I can touch my feet.

ALL. (*Imitate her as best they can.*) Tooochhhh . . . Feetz . . . (*Etc.*)

WASTBA. This is working! Oh my dear God! (*Laughs.*) I can touch my knees!

ALL. I can touch my knees . . . (*Etc.*)

WASTBA. I can touch my nose!

ALL. I can touch my nose! (*Etc.*)

WASTBA. (*She stops them. They wait, fingers on noses.*) Just hang on a minute . . . this is truly exciting. (*She looks at book again, reading.*) "You will lead them to try to touch the ceiling. When they cannot, they will, of their own volition, offer: 'I cannot touch the ceiling.' And then you will have succeeded in teaching the primary English class." (*Looks up.*) Do you understand that? (*Reading.*) "Command them to touch the wall . . . " (*Looks up.*) Touch the wall! I command you . . . (*No response. She reads again.*) . . . "and then act on your own command, leading them." (*Looks up.*) Okay. Touch the wall! (*She leads them to wall, waving arms for them to follow action and words.*) I can touch the wall!

ALL. I can tooch wall . . . I toochy wall . . . Eye tooch vall . . . (*Etc. Wastba will lead them around room, as group, screaming at them to touch various points and objects. Mulleimer will follow, but always several beats behind rest of class.*)

WASTBA. Touch the floor again! (*They do.*)

ALL. (*But LaPoubelle.*) I can touch floor again . . .

LAPOUBELLE. Ah, c'est facile. (*Swaggers.*) Zee flooor again. Voila!

WASTBA. Touch the corner!

ALL. (*Ganging together at corner.*) I can tooch corner! . . . (*Etc.*)

WASTBA. Touch your elbow!

ALL. I can tooch my elbow! (*They do. Patumiera embraces Wastba from behind, grasping her elbow.*)

PATUMIERA. I can touch your elbow! (*Wastba giggles.*)

WASTBA. Stand by, my darling students, because here it comes! (*She staggers, giggling, to C. She points to ceiling and screams to them.*) Touch the ceiling! (*She pretends to try, stretching up high above her head toward ceiling. She wags her head "NO."*) Touch the ceiling! NAW-NAW-NAW . . . ceiling. (*They all strain toward ceiling in attempt to please her, but none can touch ceiling, which is, of course, high above them. They all strain and moan.*)

ALL.	WASTBA.
Arggghhh . . .	Touch the ceiling! Ooooo . . .
Ohhhh . . .	Touch the ceiling! Ooooo . . .
Zeiling . . .	Touch the ceiling! Ooooo . . . (*Etc.*)
Arghhh . . .	

(*Etc. Mulleimer, silently, at front of room, has climbed to the top of Wastba's desk. He reaches up and touches the ceiling.*)

MULLEIMER. I . . . can . . . touch . . . zeeling . . . (*He stands, fingertips on ceiling, grinning broadly. Keeping his fingers on ceiling, he smiles down to Wastba for approval. All others in class applaud Mulleimer's success.*)

ALL. Yayy . . . Ooooo . . . (*Etc.*)

WASTBA. (*Outraged; screams at Mulleimer.*) You rotten little son of a bitch!

MULLEIMER. Zeeling?

WASTBA. (*Screams.*) Get down! (*He does; totally bewildered. She yells, as she slaps her textbook.*) There's nothing in here about Germans!

55

YOKO. Doshite ikenaindesuka? Tenjo ni sawaretanoni.

WASTBA. *(Yells, cutting Yoko's line.) SHUT IT UP!!! (There is silence in the room. Patumiera smiles at Yoko and then at Wastba, as if trying to explain the problem.)*

PATUMIERA. Eeengleesh . . . Parla Eeengleesh.

WASTBA. Oh yuh sure. You got it, champ!

PATUMIERA. *(Smiling even more broadly now.)* Eeeengleesh, si?

WASTBA. Right. Now put a little cheese and tomato sauce on that!

PATUMIERA. *(Thinks he's succeeding.)* Si?

WASTBA. *(Tight-lipped control.)* Look, my dear touristies, we could really roll up our sleeves and get down to good hard work, or I could just send you back the word "English" and you could go on saying "Eeeengliiish," just like we were playing ping-pong. *(Pauses. A knock is heard at door. Suddenly Wastba stiffens.)* Oh, my God! *(All watch her.)* Pong! *(All look from one to the other. Wastba goes to the door and, cautiously, she cracks open door. Wastba slams the door and leans against it.)* Him! Him! Him! Him! My heart! My God! Him!

ALL. *(Mimic her.)* Him?

WASTBA. Out the door. In the hall. On his feet.

ALL. Feet!

WASTBA. Crap! *(They will each pick up her word "crap" in their own accents and pass the word from one to the other, as a small ball thrown, rapidly.)*

MULLEIMER. *(Mimics her.)* Crahrp?

LAPOUBELLE. *(Mimics Mulleimer.)* Crêpe?

PATUMIERA. *(Mimics LaPoubelle.)* Cheptz?

MULLEIMER. *(Mimics Patumiera.)* Grepz?

LAPOUBELLE. *(Mimics Mulleimer.)* Greque?

PATUMIERA. Grekzi?

WASTBA. Grekzi?

PATUMIERA. Grekzi?

YOKO. Grassi?

WASTBA. Grassy?

MULLEIMER. Was?

WASTBA. Huh?

LAPOUBELLE. Hein?

YOKO. Nani?

WASTBA. Huh?

MULLEIMER. Was?

WASTBA. Huh?
MULLEIMER. Was?
WASTBA. What?
MULLEIMER. Huh?
WASTBA. (*Stands; moves to her desk.*) Listen, class, we've got to improve.
ALL. Improve!
WASTBA. If that old lady wants illicit sex, that's her business! We're here to learn English and that is, God damn it, precisely what I intend to do: so get ready to learn! (*All smile. Blank stares all around.*) What did you all come here for if you don't speak any English? This is an English-speaking country!
YOKO. Ingrish.
WASTBA. Will you just shut it up, dopey!
YOKO. (*Correcting her.*) Yoko.
WASTBA. Okay?
YOKO. (*Chirps happily.*) O-kay . . . (*Giggles.*)
WASTBA. (*Pauses.*) I'm going to explain very slowly and carefully exactly what's going on here, so listen.
PATUMIERA. Non capisco un cavolo di quel che dici.
WASTBA. (*Furiously.*) Sit down and put a belt on it, you! *Sit!*
ALL. Sit. Sitz. Seetz. (*Etc. There is a pause as all settle into their chairs. Wastba sits now in the chair behind her desk and folds her hands demurely. She is trying desperately to be calm.*) Class? (*All have notebooks and pencils poised now, thinking the lesson is finally coming.*) In the simplest possible terms, here it is: there seems to be a maniac in the hall. (*Smiles.*) Okay?
YOKO. O-kay. (*Giggles.*)
WASTBA. You think a maniac is funny? (*Yoko giggles. Wastba adds tersely.*) If I were Oriental, I would be ashamed of you. (*Yoko takes her cue from Wastba's tone of voice and is silent now.*) Right. In this particular city, we have a perfect balance between maniacs and non-maniacs: one-to-one. (*Looks up quietly.*) Here's the God's-honest truth. (*Pauses.*) My . . . well . . . cousin . . . My cousin was . . . well . . . How can I say it gently? Molested. Yup. (*Looks up.*) Did any of you know that? (*Smiles ironically.*) Or course not. You want to know why not? Because nobody knew! Not for five years now! (*Pauses; adjusts her hands on desk to gain competent, serious posture. Smiles again, ironically.*) Because she was too goddamn frightened to tell any-

body. *You know why??? . . .* uhh . . . My cousin. (*Directly to class. Wastba is anxious now; speaks quickly.*) Here's why. On the night she was molested, she crawled out of the park . . . ripped and ravished . . . interfered with . . . Yuh, that's right! . . . . She crawled out of the park and stopped the first passing man. A thin, ordinary-looking man. He was Caucasian, for Christ's sake! (*She is obviously overwrought now, fighting back her tears.*) "Help!" she said. "I've been molested!" she said. "Get a cop!" she said. "Hurry!" she said. "Please," she said. "For God's sakes," she said. "Hurry!" she said . . . (*Pauses.*) He hurried all right. You know what he did? (*Leans back; smiles bravely.*) *He molested me.* (*All are staring blankly at her.*) No comments? No words of sympathy? No "Tough break, kiddo?" (*Pauses.*) I could dial "Weather" and get a bigger response than I'm getting from you! (*All continue to stare blankly.*)

LAPOUBELLE. (*Quietly. He is completely perplexed.*) Chère mademoiselle . . . écoutez . . . Je suis absolument désolé d'avoir dire ça, mais il faut que vous . . .

WASTBA. (*To LaPoubelle, contemptuously.*) I s'pose you think that's suave? Maybe that works in Brussels, froggy, but it's not cutting any ice with me, okay?

LAPOUBELLE. Personne ne comprend rien . . . *personne!*

WASTBA. Did it ever occur to any of you that your mothers were women?

PATUMIERA. Aspetta un momento. (*He has been studying his phrasebook and writing notes onto his pad of paper. He smiles proudly at Yoko. He smiles quietly at Wastba, who is blowing her nose. All eyes on Patumiera now.*) . . . un momento. Diro qualcosa . . . (*He holds his pad in front of him and studies it. He smiles again.*) . . . Momento . . . (*Rummages through his phrasebook; smiles constantly to Yoko.*)

TRANSLATOR. Wait just a minute. I'll say something.

PATUMIERA. Solo un secondo!

TRANSLATOR. Just a second.

PATUMIERA. (*Finds a phrase he likes.*) Ne ho uno!

TRANSLATOR. I've got one! (*Patumiera slithers to Wastba, using his most practiced movie-star walk. He has memorized something from his phrasebook. Wastba is unhappy. She senses that Patumiera has some words of consolation, hence, she looks up at him.*)

PATUMIERA. (*Reads slowly.*) **Signorina, may . . . I . . .** smork?

WASTBA. *Smork?*

PATUMIERA. Posso fumare, signorina? (*Again, in English. Tries new pronunciation of word this time.*) May . . . eye . . . schmork? (*He waves his cigarette pack.*) Sigaretta!

WASTBA. Oh, sure, swell, smork. All of you, go on! You want to have sets of malignant lungs: go on! Light up! Enjoy! Have your sigaretti . . .

PATUMIERA. (*Correcting her.*) Sigaretta! (*Smiles to all.*)

WASTBA. Sigaretta! (*Patumiera smiles, shrugs, lights up a cigarette, drags on it deeply, blows smoke into room. He will soon offer cigarettes to all, who will in turn begin to smoke. As each is quite anxious, quite a lot of smoke will be produced. Soon, in fact, the room will be filled with smoke and Wastba will be coughing. At the moment, Wastba is writing the words "Basic Salutations" on blackboard.*)

PATUMIERA. (*Offers cigarettes to Yoko.*) Sigaretta?

YOKO. Jie kekko desu. Watashinoga arimasukara. (*She lights a Japanese cigarette.*)

PATUMIERA. (*To Mulleimer.*) Sigaretta?

MULLEIMER. Nein, danke. Ich habe meine eigenen. (*He lights a German cigarette.*)

PATUMIERA. Si, Eigenen . . . (*To LaPoubelle.*) Sigaretta?

LAPOUBELLE. Non merci, j'ai ma pipe. (*He lights a French pipe.*)

YOKO. Ie kekko desu. Watashinoga arimasunode. (*She waves her Japanese cigarette.*)

PATUMIERA. Giapponese, quella sigaretta? Vuole cambiare?

TRANSLATOR. Japanese, that cigarette? Let's exchange . . .

YOKO. Sorewa Itaria no tabako?

TRANSLATOR. Is that an Italian cigarette?

MULLEIMER. (*He offers LaPoubelle a drag of his cigarette.*) Wollen Sie mal meine probieren? Vielleicht zu stark fuer Sie . . .

LAPOUBELLE. J'essaierai le vôtre, et vous le mien. Quoique le tabac francais sera probablement trop fort pour vous . . . (*He takes Mulleimer's cigarette and puffs on it, exchanging his pipe for cigarette.*)

TRANSLATOR. I'll try yours, you try mine. French tobacco's probably too strong for you though . . .

YOKO. Omoshiroi kedo. Yowai desune.

TRANSLATOR. Interesting, but too weak for my taste . . .

PATUMIERA. Interessante, ma un po leggiere per me. (*Puffing away happily.*)

TRANSLATOR. Interesting, but too weak for my taste . . .

MULLEIMER. Ganz interessant, aber etwas schwach fuer meinen Geschmack. (*Puffing away happily.*)

TRANSLATOR. Interesting, but too weak for my taste . . .

LAPOUBELLE. Interessant, mais pas assez fort à mon goût. (*Puffing away happily.*)

TRANSLATOR. Interesting, but too weak for my taste . . . (*The room is full of smoke. Wastba is gasping and coughing. Patumiera walks to her, offers his packette of cigarettes.*)

PATUMIERA. Sigaretta?

WASTBA. Oh, c'mon, will you? (*They all puff away, smiling.*) I would like your . . . (*Coughs.*) . . . attention . . . (*Coughs.*) There is a slight problem. (*Coughs again. Room is full of smoke.*) For Christ's sake! (*She slaps at the smoke in the air.*) Open something, will you? (*Wastba staggers to door and opens it, trying to add fresh air into room. She opens door fully, hiding herself behind door a moment. Mrs. Pong is just outside door, smiling, re-entering room. She is puffing away on a Chinese cigarette. She takes step on to threshold. All class members see Mrs. Pong. Wastba does not, as she is behind door. Suddenly Wastba, remembering that there is danger outside of door, slams door in Mrs. Pong's face, knocking her out of threshold and sight. All are astonished.*)

LAPOUBELLE. Elle vient de claquer la porte au nez de cette vieille Malasienne! (*He nervously puffs his pipe.*)

PATUMIERA. Credo che sia stata lei ad uccidere la vecchia giapponese (*To Wastba.*) Mi scusi, ma credo che lei ha appena ucciso la signora giapponese.

WASTBA. I know. I know. You must think I'm crazy to have opened the door with that maniac out there, but the smoke in here is so goddamned thick! (*Smiles, coughs.*) Please stop smoking, okay?

YOKO. (*Puffing away on cigarette nervously.*) Sensei wa toshi-yorino gofu in o kizutsuke mashitayo.

WASTBA. Please, stop your smoking, okay, Yokè? (*Yoko smiles and puffs. Smoke hits Wastba's face. Wastba takes her cigarette and drops it on the floor. Angrily.)* For God's sakes! I asked you politely!

YOKO. Toshiyori no gofujin o kizutsukete tabako o fumitsukete. Watashi wa seki ni modorimasu.

PATUMIERA. *(Confused.)* Sigaretta? *(He offers cigarette to Wastba.)*

WASTBA. Oh, shove it, will you?

MULLEIMER. *(Puffing away on cigarette, he blows smoke right into Wastba's face.)* Ich lasse sie herein. *(Wastba grabs his cigarette.)* Hallo!

WASTBA. *(She stomps cigarette out on floor.)* That's just about enough, okay?

MULLEIMER. Was ist denn? *(Wastba has begun to snap. She will scream at each of them, until she will suddenly say, in the sweetest of tones, good morning.)*

WASTBA. Sit down, Pilsner!

MULLEIMER. Wie, bitte?

WASTBA. *Down! Sit!* *(He sits.)*

PATUMIERA. Non capisco nemmeno una parola di quel che sta dicendo.

WASTBA. Shut your mouth!

LAPOUBELLE. Excusez-moi, s'il vous plaît, mais . . .

WASTBA. *(Screams.)* All of you: listen! *(Silence in room. N.B. Change in her tone will be complete. She moves two steps into the center of the room, clasps her hands together and smiles demurely.)* Good morning. *(No response. She nods to LaPoubelle.)* Good morning. *(She rolls her arms at him, motioning for him to follow her words: to repeat them.)* Good morning.

LAPOUBELLE. *(Stands; in disbelief.)* Goood morr-ning.

WASTBA. Perfect. *(To Mulleimer, who stands. Lapoubelle sits.)* Now you. *(He stares dumbly at her.)* Good morning.

MULLEIMER. Gud morgan . . .

WASTBA. Morning . . .

MULLEIMER. Morging . . .

WASTBA. Morning!

MULLEIMER. Morning!

WASTBA. You see? You got a will, you got a way. *(To Yoko, after Mulleimer sits.)* Right?

YOKO. *(Yoko stands for her turn. She turns to Patumiera and whispers.)* Good morning, eh? *(Patumiera nods.)*

61

WASTBA. Okay, let's start you right out on the other essential
. . . according to my plan. (*Smiles to Yoko.*) Good night.
PATUMIERA *and* YOKO. Ohh.
WASTBA. Good night!
YOKO. Good nightie.
WASTBA. Good nightie! Is that supposed to be cute? Good
nightie! (*Smiles ironically.*) It's not "Good nightie" but "Good
night." (*Motions to her to repeat words.*) Good night. (*No re-
sponse. She speaks the words again, but with tremendous hostility.*)
Good night!
YOKO. (*Repeats tone.*) Good night!
WASTBA. (*To Patumiera.*) What's funny?
PATUMIERA. Good night.
WASTBA. What's funny? I asked what's funny? . . .
PATUMIERA. (*Shyly now.*) Good night?
LAPOUBELLE. (*Leans in correcting Patumiera, smiling to
Wastba for approval.*) Goooood night. (*Smiles again. Nods
smugly.*) Goooood night.
WASTBA. You've got yourself a horrid oooo-sound. (*She
squeezes his lips.*) Gud, gud, gud. Gud night.
LAPOUBELLE. (*Repeats exactly.*) Gud night.
MULLEIMER. (*Leans in to correct LaPoubelle at the same time
Patumiera and Yoko try the same words.*) Guden, guden, guden.
Guden night.
YOKO. Good nightie . . .
PATUMIERA. God naght . . .   (*Together—
MULLEIMER. Guden, guden, guden . . . (*They*   4 *times.*)
each continue as LaPoubelle goes into a rage.)
LAPOUBELLE. C'est une catastrophe, cette leçon . . . et c'est
de votre faute, je crois . . .
WASTBA. *Silence!*
MULLEIMER. (*Angrily now, to Wastba.*) Ich komme micht mit.
Tut mir leid, aber ich verstehe nicht was Sie sagen . . .
WASTBA. (*Screams.*) I can't stand it! (*All stop talking and look
at her.*) Stop your goddamn babble! Stop! Stop! Stop! (*She
stands.*) I demand you stop! (*She sits in Mrs. Pong's chair.*) I'm
upset. (*She begins rocking Mrs. Pong's desk back and forth,
moaning.*) Oh dear God, I'm upset . . . My heart is filled with
such loathing for all of you! (*Her body heaves as she sobs.
Patumiera walks to her, cautiously.*)

PATUMIERA. Come si sente? Sta bene?

WASTBA. (*On hearing his Italian language, sobs all the more.*) It's hopeless, hopeless . . .

PATUMIERA. Che t' è successo? Diccelo per favore. (*Patumiera touches Wastba's arm and she pulls back, violently, and screams.*)

WASTBA. Don't you touch me! Oh, you would touch me! (*She is on her feet now.*)

PATUMIERA. Per amor del cielo!

WASTBA. Don't you know? Can't you tell?? (*Pauses; no response.*) Look at me! (*Nods ironically.*) Don't pretend it doesn't show. (*No response.*) Okay. Okay . . . (*Stands erect.*) This is my first class, too . . . They just called me last night. (*Waits for reaction. Gets none. Smiles, nods.*) Shocked, huh? Well . . . now you know . . . We must not fail here. (*Pauses.*) You fail and I fail. I fail and you fail. You fail and I fail and we all fail. I fail and you don't get to speak English. You fail and I don't get to teach English. We all fail and . . . (*Pauses.*) You see now, don't you? Language could be our mutual Waterloo! (*Pauses.*) Have I made myself perfectly clear?

YOKO. (*Smiling.*) Ware-ware wa ittai anataga doshte . . .

WASTBA. (*Screams.*) I'm gonna stuff an eggroll in that mouth of yours, butterfly! (*Silence.*) The next three words out of my mouth will be the most important words in the English language. (*She has been holding her lesson plan book and leafing through it. Her calmness at this moment is icy.*) I certainly hope you'll have the decency to pay attention. (*She stares at her class. All look from one to another, wondering what it was they did that drove Wastba crazy. Suddenly we hear three enormously loud raps at the door. The sound is quite terrifying.*)

SMIEDNIK. (*Off-stage. His lines are intercut with the pounding.*) Daj mi moja miotᴤe, pani! Hey, Sᴪodka, bez mej moitᴪy nie moje pracowac! Nie zartuję, panno, dawaj miotᴤe i dawaj ją szybkó. Wchodzę!! Otwieraj cholerne dzwi! (*There is a sharp intake of breath from all and then silence. Wastba looks at class, bows head, speaks softly.*)

WASTBA. Poor, poor Pong. (*She walks to Mrs. Pong's desk and gathers the four takeout containers together in a stack. She returns to the front of the room and drops the four takeout containers into the wastebasket.*)

LAPOUBELLE. Nom de Dieu, qu'est-ce que c'est que-ça?

TRANSLATOR. What the hell is that?

PATUMIERA. Che é successo?

TRANSLATOR. What's happening?

YOKO. Dare ka hairitagatte irunjanaidesuka?

TRANSLATOR. I think somebody's trying to get into the room.

MULLEIMER. Was zum Teufel war das? (*Pauses; moves up from his seat.*) Was zum *Jeufel* war das? (*Moves to Wastba.*)

TRANSLATOR. What the devil was that?

PATUMIERA. (*Moves to Wastba.*) Che è successo, signorina?

LAPOUBELLE. (*Moves to Wastba.*) Qu'est-ce que c'est, mademoiselle?

WASTBA. Please, take your seats now . . . (*Smiles, calmly.*) All of you: sit down. Come on, now . . . (*Calmly.*) Please sit down.

MULLEIMER. Wir mussen die Tür aufmachen, und nachsehen, Fräulein. (*Mulleimer moves to the door. Wastba hurls her body between Mulleimer and the door.*) Heh! (*Mulleimer hops away from her, moving backwards.*)

WASTBA. Sit!

MULLEIMER. Fräulein, bitte . . .

WASTBA. J am the captain of this ship . . . not you! (*Backs him away from door by screaming and moving forward. Mulleimer continues to hop.*)

MULLEIMER. Fraulein!

WASTBA. J'm the one who killed the morning preparing . . . not you! (*Moves forward again.*)

MULLEIMER. (*Hops backward again.*) Fräulein!

WASTBA. J'm responsible here . . . not you!

YOKO. (*Jo LaPoubelle.*) Ittai do shitandesuka?

LAPOUBELLE. (*Jo Yoko as he stands.*) Qu'est-ce qu'elle fait?

PATUMIERA. (*Stands.*) Che sta facendo?

LAPOUBELLE. (*Jo Wastba.*) Quand ce navire coulera, je serai le premier rat à se sauver.

WASTBA. We've got to stick together! (*Screams; panicked.*) We've got to stick together. (*Yells at Mulleimer.*) Sit down and stick together.

MULLEIMER. Ich rühr mich nicht bis ich weiss was da draussen passiert ist!

WASTBA. (*Screams.*) Jake your seats!

PATUMIERA. *(He recognizes phrase and repeats same, screaming word aloud trying to be helpful.)* Teetz . . .

WASTBA. I beg your pardon?

PATUMIERA. *(Pounds his desk; motions to all seats in room.)* Goood teetz . . .

WASTBA. Mister, do you know that I am an educated woman? I may be Business Administration and not Language Arts, which is only to say that while words may not be my way . . . my field . . . I am nonetheless degree-certified and educated. Furthermore, this is not a goddamn Latin country! We are civilized people here! Now, goddammit, *sit down!* *(Suddenly there is the sound of pounding on the door again.)*

SMIEDNIK. *(Screams off-stage; screams are intercut with the pounding at the door.)* Potreba mi mej miotѰy, kochanie. Pani, musze, iśc̀ dp domu. Wchodze̜! Otwieraj cholerne dzwi! *(Silence in the room again. LaPoubelle speaks first, under his breath. He is quite obviously frightened.)*

LAPOUBELLE. *Mais, enfin, merde, alors!* . . . *Qu'est-ce que c'est que ça???* *La Guerre, Madame?* . . .

WASTBA. *(Intensely.)* Don't you understand that there is more of us than there is of him?

MULLEIMER. *Was ist passiert, Fraeulein? Kriegsausbruch vielleicht?*

PATUMIERA. *Che è successo, signorina? Una battaglia?*

WASTBA. He's probably only just another poor demented lunatic needing money for Godknowswhat kind of drug . . . That's all . . . It makes me want to spit. *Ptwew!* *(She actually spits on floor.)*

PATUMIERA. Signorina . . . *Vietato sputare,* eh?

WASTBA. Money!

PATUMIERA. Money!

WASTBA. Money! That's it! Money!

YOKO. *(Repeats word as well.)* . . . money . . . *(Giggles.)*

WASTBA. *(Grabbing her pocketbook.)* I'll chip in a dollar if you at will . . . *(Looks up at them.)* We can buy him off!

LAPOUBELLE. Mais, ma chère mademoiselle, il faut que vous nous donniez juste une petite chance, alors! . . . Nous sommes . . .

WASTBA. A dollar! *(To Patumiera.)* A dollar, you!

PATUMIERA. *(With dollar, proudly.)* Dollarr. *(She grabs his dollar.)* Eyyy!

65

WASTBA. Thank you. (*To LaPoubelle.*) C'mon, moustache,* it's your life or a rotten dollar! What's to think about? Gimme' a dollar.

LAPOUBELLE. (*He takes out his wallet. She grabs it and takes a dollar.*) Madame!

WASTBA. I'm only taking a dollar. One. See? (*To Yoko.*) You paying attention? Hello?

YOKO. (*Has a dollar now.*) Hello . . . Dolly.

WASTBA. To know you is to love you . . . Gimme' . . . (*Takes the dollar, counts people and then money.*) Who's not in? (*To Mulleimer.*) You! A dollar. (*He takes out dollar.*)

MULLEIMER. Dollar, ja . . .

WASTBA. Good boy.

MULLEIMER. (*Proudly.*) Okay. (*Wastba walks carefully to the door. All are frozen to see what will happen. She puts her hand on the doorknob.*)

WASTBA. Five lousy bucks. Let's hope he's got a sense of humor. Get the picture? (*She looks at Mulleimer.*) Hey! (*Grabs camera from him.*) That'll help.

MULLEIMER. Ääh . . . Das ist meine Yashika, Fräulein . . .

WASTBA. (*To Yoko.*) Okay, Yoko. (*Pauses; amazed.*) Just wait a goddam minute . . . (*To Yoko.*) Did you know that "Yoko" is "okay" spelled backwards. (*Pauses.*) I'm wrong . . . (*Pauses.*) . . . Okay is "yako." You're Yoko. (*"Yako" should be made to rhyme with "Jack-o." Pauses; again in panic.*) Something of value! I need something of value! (*Sees Yoko's gold make-up case.*) Gimme' that! (*Grabs for it. Yoko resists.*)

YOKO. Aiiii . . .

WASTBA. Gimme'! Make-up case!

YOKO. (*Resisting.*) Aayyy-iiii . . .

WASTBA. Make-up casey!

YOKO. (*Suddenly giggles.*) May cupcasey . . . (*Gives over make-up case to Wastba.*)

WASTBA. Six hundred million more of you, huh? That's just swell. (*Moves to door.*) Well, let's hope, right? (*Cracks door open a bit. LaPoubelle grabs umbrella for protection. Stands by his desk with umbrella raised over his head.*) I'll try what I assume is his tongue . . . Couldn't hurt. (*Yells out door.*) Me voy a lavar un poco para quitarme la arena que tengo pegada! (*And with that she throws money, make-up case and camera out of door into the hall-*

*If he is moustached; otherwise, baldy, shorty, whatever.

66

way. *She instantly slams the door closed. All are shocked and amazed and scream at her.*)

ALL. (*In own language.*) Hey! What the hell did you do! That was my dollar! Have you lost your mind? (*Etc. Mulleimer moves to the door. His attitude is "I'll take care of this."*)

MULLEIMER. (*To all.*) Sit. (*To Wastba.*) Heute meine Brille und meine Yashika; morgen was? *Meine Schuhe? Meine Hosen?* Was, Fräulein, was?

WASTBA. Stay back, I'm telling you. (*Raises her fist.*) I'm not above throwing a punch!

MULLEIMER. Das ist doch lacherlich.

WASTBA. I told you that we have to stick together and you GODDAMMIT! are going to have to *stick!* (*And with that, she punches his shoulder. Her fist is to Mulleimer's shoulder what a mosquito is to a grazing cow.*)

MULLEIMER. Was machen Sie da, meine Dame?

WASTBA. My hand! (*She is bent in pain.*) My poor hand. (*She moves to her desk.*) I really hurt my hand on you.

MULLEIMER. Was ist passiert?

YOKO. Doshitanodes'ka?

LAPOUBELLE. Mais. Qu'est-ce qui est arrivé?

PATUMIERA. Che è successo?

WASTBA. (*Crying.*) I really hurt my hand on you . . .

MULLEIMER. Warum haben sie mich geschlagen?

YOKO. Senseiwa naze Doitsujin o naguttan desuka?

LAPOUBELLE. Pourquoi elle lui a tapé dessus?

PATUMIERA. Perché gli ha dato quella botta?

WASTBA. I'm upset!

PATUMIERA. Sono sturbato, Io!

WASTBA. I'm so upset!

MULLEIMER. Bin ganz ausser mich. (*He paces, as a cat, the length of the room, holding eye-contact with Wastba.*)

YOKO. Iyani nacchau wa.

WASTBA. Am I ever upset!

YOKO. Honto ni iyani nacchau wa.

WASTBA. (*Sobbing.*) Oh, God! I'm upset!

MULLEIMER. Mein Gott! Ich bin ausser mich!

WASTBA. This is truly upsetting. I want you to know that this is truly very upsetting.

MULLEIMER. (*He stands, throws notebooks on the floor; gathers his belongings.*) Fraeulein, ich geh' nach Hause. (*Mulleimer moves to door; stops. He turns and faces Wastba.*)

TRANSLATOR. I'm going home now, Lady!

MULLEIMER. Aber bevor ich geh', will ich Ihnen noch was sagen . . .

TRANSLATOR'S VOICE. But before I go, I gotta' tell you something . . .

MULLEIMER. Frueher dachte ich, dass Tod durch Ersticken das Schlimmste sie.

TRANSLATOR'S VOICE. I used to think that death by suffocation would be the worst.

MULLEIMER. Hab' mich geirrt.

TRANSLATOR'S VOICE. I was wrong.

MULLEIMER. (*He puts on his cap and coat.*) Sie sind das Schlimmste.

TRANSLATOR'S VOICE. *You* are the worst.

MULLEIMER. Tod durch Ersticken ist ein Stueck Apfelstrudel verlichen zu einem abend mit Ihnen . . .

TRANSLATOR'S VOICE. Death by suffocation is a piece of apple strudel next to a night with you . . .

MULLEIMER. Ich verlasse diese klasse, bevor ich meinen Verstand und meine Schuhe verliere.

TRANSLATOR'S VOICE. I'm getting out of here while I still have my mind and my shoes.

MULLEIMER. Und wenn Ihr Freund der "mugger" sie haben will, kann er sie haben. (*He moves to her desk.*)

TRANSLATOR. If your friend the "mugger" wants them, he can have them.

MULLEIMER. Was Ihr kostbares Englisch anbelangt . . . (*He rubs his hand through words written on blackboard.*)

TRANSLATOR. As for your precious English . . .

MULLEIMER. . . . So platzieren Sie es auf einen kleinen, aber eleganten stuhl . . .

TRANSLATOR. . . . stick it on the center of a small but elegant chair . . .

MULLEIMER. (*He pulls her chair out and motions to seat, on his line.*) . . . und sit! (*Pauses. Goes to door.*) Fraulein . . . Auf Wiedersehn. (*He bows, clicks his heels. All freeze for a moment. Mulleimer exits. He leaves door open. All stare a moment.*)

WASTBA. (*Realizes, yells to Patumiera.*) Close that door! (*She*

68

stands straight.) Close that door! (*She rushes to door.*) Close that door! (*She slams it closed.*) Oh, God! (*All stare, amazed.*)

LAPOUBELLE. Elle a fermé la porte à l'Allemand!

PATUMIERA. Dov'e lo Svizzero?

YOKO. Sensei wa doitsujin o Shimedashimashita!

WASTBA. Okay, everybody, just settle!

PATUMIERA. Hai sbattuto fuori lo Svizzero!

WASTBA. (*To Patumiera.*) Settle, you!

YOKO. (*Screams, to Wastba.*) Sensei wa doitsujin o shimedashimashita! (*Sound of knocking at the door.*)

LAPOUBELLE. Ecoutez!

WASTBA. Back to your seat.

LAPOUBELLE. Il a quelqu'un qui frappe a la porte, Madame!

WASTBA. Sit, will you? (*Knocking at the door again.*)

PATUMIERA. Senti, forse e' lo Svizzero, no? (*Stands, looks to Wastba.*) Non dovremmo aprire la porta?

YOKO. Doitsujin wa hairitagatteirun ja nai desuka.

WASTBA. Settle, everybody, just settle!

LAPOUBELLE. (*Moving forward in room.*) Vaut mieux aller voir. (*He carries his umbrella for protection. The sound of knocking at the door.*) Ecoutez!

WASTBA. Go back to your seat! (*The sound of pounding at the door.*) I said "Back to your seat!" (*The sound of pounding at the door.*)

LAPOUBELLE. Je vais ouvrir la porte.

WASTBA. It's your funeral. (*She steps back from the door, smiling and nodding magnanimously. LaPoubelle holds his umbrella as a club against door.*)

LAPOUBELLE. Qui est là? (*Suddenly we hear the sound of three enormous pounding sounds, joined by hard knocking. LaPoubelle jams his umbrella against door to hold it closed; Yoko hides behind a frightened Patumiera. The door rattles under the pounding.*)

SMIEDNIK. (*Off-stage; screaming. His screams are intercut with enormous knockings of the pail against the door.*) Pani, muszę iść do domu! Nie zaetuję, panno, dawaj miotłe i dawaj ją szybkó. Wchodze! Otwieraj cholerne dżwi! (*LaPoubelle is frozen in his tracks; there is silence. LaPoubelle finally backs away and hides near his desk.*)

WASTBA. Now, perhaps, you'll take me seriously. (*Pauses.*) You're all . . . well . . . new to this, while I'm . . . well . . .

69

not new to this (*Pauses. Smiles.*) Please, everybody . . . sit down.

LAPOUBELLE. Ils sont dans de beaux draps . . . le Suisse et la vieille Hawaienne, aussi. (*Bows head.*) C'est certain maintenant . . . Mon Dieu.

TRANSLATOR. The Swiss and the old Hawaiian lady are in big trouble. My God, that's for sure.

WASTBA. (*Condescending tone.*) Yes . . . I know . . . It's never what our parents told us it would be. (*Touches LaPoubelle's shoulder.*) Please sit down now, okay?

LAPOUBELLE. No seet.

WASTBA. Sit!

LAPOUBELLE. Non!

WASTBA. Yes!

LAPOUBELLE. Non. No seet!

WASTBA. Damn you!

LAPOUBELLE. Ne me touchez pas! (*Shakes loose from her. Moves to his seat. Stops. Smiles at her ironically.*) Tu es dingue, cherie . . . mais adorable . . . (*Waves.*) Je t'embrasse . . . (*Pause.*) Mon Dieu. Ma tête. Mon cul . . .

WASTBA. You're going to have to stop wagging that tongue of yours . . .

LAPOUBELLE. (*Suddenly screams.*) Je n'ai plus confiance en vous, mademoiselle. *Je vous deteste!*

WASTBA. I'm going to have to treat you like a child. (*She walks to LaPoubelle.*) Every time you speak your tongue instead of English . . . (*She slaps his hand.*) I'll slap you.

LAPOUBELLE. Pourquoi avez-vous fait ça? (*Wastba slaps La-Poubelle again.*)

PATUMIERA. Perche' t'ha preso a schiaffi?

WASTBA. (*To Patumiera.*) There's that tongue of yours now!

PATUMIERA. Eh?

WASTBA. I'll have to slap you, too. (*She slaps Patumiera.*) Okay?

PATUMIERA. (*He reacts as a movie star might for these lines.*) Non picchio mai una donna. Anche se ti sorprende, essendo io Italiano . . .

WASTBA. You're not learning . . .

PATUMIERA. (*He moves now as a movie star might for these words.*) Eh, Signora! . . . Io . . .

YOKO. Chotto kiite kudasai!

70

WASTBA. You, too? (*Walks to Yoko.*) Sorry. (*Slaps Yoko's hand.*)

YOKO. Cho-to!

PATUMIERA. E' pazza! (*Wastba slaps Patumiera's face.*)

LAPOUBELLE. Je m'en vais. (*LaPoubelle stands. Wastba slaps him.*) Elle est completement cinglée! (*She slaps him again, violently now.*) Bordel! (*She slaps him again. He looks to Patumiera.*) J'en ai assez! (*LaPoubelle begins to pack his belongings as rapidly as he can. He stuffs papers and notebooks and clothing into his briefcases and bookbags. He is now hysterical. Wastba, equally hysterical, will slap him whenever she hears French language being emitted from LaPoubelle's lips.*) Faites ce que vous voudrez, moi, je m'en vais.

TRANSLATOR'S VOICE. I couldn't care less what you're after here . . . I'm getting out! (*Wastba slaps LaPoubelle. N.B. He is now slapped both for his own words and for the Translator's words.*)

LAPOUBELLE. J'en ai assez!

TRANSLATOR'S VOICE. I've had enough! (*Wastba slaps LaPoubelle again. Wastba slaps LaPoubelle twice.*)

LAPOUBELLE. Madame, votre anglais, vous n'avez qu'à vous en farcir. (*Wastba slaps him.*)

TRANSLATOR'S VOICE. Lady, you can take your English and eat it! (*Wastba slaps him again.*)

LAPOUBELLE. Maintenant, il faut absolument que je m'en aille. (*Wastba slaps him again.*)

TRANSLATOR'S VOICE. Now I'm *really* leaving!

LAPOUBELLE. Voila! (*Slap. LaPoubelle places his hand on the doorknob. Wastba pulls back from him, frightened. Silence, as all stare at LaPoubelle's back as he faces door. Suddenly, he freezes.*) Ca alors! Attendez, un petit moment . . .

TRANSLATOR'S VOICE. Uhhh, let's just wait a minute . . .

LAPOUBELLE. (*Turning back into position of facing Wastba and classmates. He has a sick grin on his face.*) Je m'en vais pas!

TRANSLATOR. I'm not gonna' leave . . .

LAPOUBELLE. Je perdrai mon boulot, ma jeune femme, mes enfants seraient obligés de quitter leur école privée . . .

TRANSLATOR. I'll lose my job, my young wife, and my children would have to drop out of private school . . .

LAPOUBELLE. En plus, ce con-là, il me tuerait.

TRANSLATOR. Also I'll be killed by the maniac out there.

LAPOUBELLE. (*He walks to Wastba and offers his hand for her to hit.*) S'il vout plait, mademoiselle. (*She hits his hand sharply. He clenches hand into fist, considers punching her; does not. He smiles instead. LaPoubelle now returns to his chair and sits. He has rejoined the class. All sit quietly; attentive.*)

WASTBA. Quiet, huh? (*Smiles.*) You've learned, huh? (*Smiles again and makes a sudden pronouncement.*) I have seen The Miracle Worker! (*She returns to her desk and sits. She smiles; composed and erect now.*) Calmness prevails and I am pleased. (*Smiles.*) Now then, in accordance with our lesson plan, I would like to discuss the verb "to be." (*Pauses.*) I hope this will fulfill and satisfy your foreign expectations. (*She stands and writes the words "To Be" on the blackboard next to the word "English." She has thus created the sentence "To Be English."*)

PATUMIERA. Che stai cercando di dire? (*Wastba turns and stares a moment at Patumiera, returns to blackboard. There is absolute silence in the room. Her handwriting on blackboard is mere scribbles; almost more like Japanese characters than English.*)

WASTBA. (*Speaks words as she writes.*) I am. You are. He, she, it is. We are. You are. They are. (*Smiles.*) How many of you know this already? (*Absolute silence in the room.*) Nobody. (*Stands; writes phrases on blackboard; turns to class after each and reads. She calls for the class to repeat her words, slapping each word with pointer for emphasis.*) I am. You are. He, she, it is. We are. You are. They are. (*Motions with arms for them to follow.*) Repeat after me, please. (*Smiles and points to blackboard.*) I am.

ALL. I am.

WASTBA. You are.

ALL. You are.

WASTBA. He, she, it is.

ALL. He, she, it is.

WASTBA. We are.

ALL. We are.

WASTBA. You are.

ALL. You are.

WASTBA. They are.

ALL. They are.

WASTBA. Good.

ALL. Good.

WASTBA. Stop!

ALL. Stop!

WASTBA. (Screams.) I said "Stop!" (LaPoubelle, who is humiliated, screams and pounds his desk, out of control.)

LAPOUBELLE. I said stop!

WASTBA. Do any of you have any questions? (Suddenly LaPoubelle stands. Smashed umbrella held as sword, he charges to the front of the room.)

LAPOUBELLE. (Stands with his belongings in his arms. He nods to Patumiera.) Bon soir, Monsieur Ravioli . . . (Nods to Yoko.) Bon Soir, ma petit Mademoiselle Sukiyaki . . . (Bows to Wastba.) . . . et au revoir, Madame le Hot Dog . . .(He unlocks door; turns again to Wastba.) . . . Au revoir, ma chère femme . . .

TRANSLATOR. Goodbye, my wife . . .

LAPOUBELLE. . . . et au revoir a mes petites enfants et vos leurs ècoles privèes . . .

TRANSLATOR. . . . and goodbye my children and goodbye your private schools . . .

LAPOUBELLE. (Prepares to leap out of door.) Salut, ange de la mort!

TRANSLATOR. Hello, Angel of Death! (LaPoubelle exits play. Wastba goes to door, closes it, locks it.)

WASTBA. I repeat: do any of you have any questions?

YOKO. (Stunned silence first.) Furansujin ga nigemashita! (She screams the same words again.) Furansujin ga nigemashita! (Patumiera, realizing Yoko will be slapped for speaking something other than English, leans in and whispers to her, using hand gestures for emphasis.)

PATUMIERA. Sta zitto o quella ti prene a botte!

WASTBA. (Thinking Patumiera is about to hit Yoko.) Hey!

PATUMIERA. Eh?

WASTBA. I'll do the slapping around here, okay? (No response. Patumiera just smiles.)

YOKO. (Hides her hands behind her back.) Furansujin ga nigemashita!

WASTBA. (To Patumiera.) Did you hear me?

YOKO. Furansujin!

WASTBA. Don't let me hear that tonque of yours again! (Pauses; raises hand.) You hear me?

YOKO. (Head bowed in guilt and shame.) Sumimaszn.

73

WASTBA. Better. (*Rubbing her hands together, walking backwards to her desk.*) I am.
PATUMIERA. (*Repeats.*) I am.
WASTBA. (*To Yoko.*) You are. (*No response.*) You are. *You are!* (*Yoko looks up, quietly.*)
YOKO. (*Pronounced perfectly.*) You . . . are.
WASTBA. (*To Patumiera.*) He, she, it is.
PATUMIERA. (*Repeats.*) He, she, it is.
WASTBA. (*To Yoko.*) We are. (*No response.*) We are. (*No response.*) I said "We are!" (*No response.*) *We are!* (*Yoko turns around to Wastba.*)
YOKO. (*Quietly smiling.*) Watashi ga Amerika ni tatta hi ni wa nihyaku-hachijunin mono hito ga eki made miokurini kitekuremashita. (*She slaps her own hand, sharply.*)
TRANSLATOR. There were two hundred and eighty people gathered at the train station waving good-bye to me on the day I left for America.
YOKO. (*She moves to position in front of Wastba.*) Sonouchino nihyaku nanaju-nananin wa itoko deshita. (*She slaps her own hand again.*)
TRANSLATOR. Two hundred and seventy-seven of them were cousins.
YOKO. (*Sits in chair next to Wastba so that Wastba cannot avoid her eyes.*) Sonouchino hitori wa watashino haha, mo hitori wa watashino chichi.
TRANSLATOR. One was my mother and one was my father.
YOKO. (*Packing.*) Nokori no hitori was boi furendo no Jun deshita.
TRANSLATOR. The other one was my boyfriend, Jun.
YOKO. America ni kurutameni watashiwa minnato wakaretano desu.
TRANSLATOR. I gave up everybody to come here.
YOKO. Kono heya kara derukoto wa nijyu-nanadai tsuzuita watashino ie no meiyo o kegasukoto ni narimasu. (*Goes to chair, collects her belongings.*)
TRANSLATOR. Walking out that front door represents more humiliation to me than the last twenty-seven generations of my family could even think about. (*Gathers belongings, nods to Patumiera to join her. Patumiera shrugs a "No." Yoko does an Italian put-down gesture. She moves to door.*)

YOKO. (*Opens door, after peeking out carefully.*) Mohito ban anatato issho ni irukurainara roka de kichigai to rumba o odotta hoga mada mashidesu. (*Turns and faces Wastba again.*)

TRANSLATOR. Sugar, I would rather dance a rhumba with the lunatic in the hall than spend another night with you.

YOKO. Sayonara, Misu American Pie. (*Yoko bows. She exits play. Smiednik bursts into room. The knees of his trousers are visibly soaked. On seeing Smiednik, Wastba will recognize him and reach a near catatonic state of fear. Patumiera is confused and frightened.*)

SMIEDNIK. Styszałaś teu kawat o Polaku i o śliwce, also teu o Polaku i ogòrku? Styszałaś o Polaku i stzajku smieciarzy?

TRANSLATOR. Heard the one about the Pollack and the prunes? Heard the one about the Pollack and the pickle? Heard the one about the Pollack and the garbage strike?

SMIEDNIK. Ty myślisz że to żarty??? Ty myślisz mnie imie Smienczne?

TRANSLATOR. You think we're all *jokes*??? Why? Just because I've got a funny name? (*Smiednik kicks wastebasket, violently.*)

SMIEDNIK. Czegòs mi miotłe ukradła? Jamuzce podłoge myc, albo sie moge sie pojytce . . . gdzie jesta?

TRANSLATOR. Why'd you steal my mop? I gotta' mop floors, lady, that's how I put the food on the table. (*Pauses.*) Where is it?

SMIEDNIK. Jednego godzina wdomu chiat byłem. Widzic sie! Na kolany I wrence, podłoge wy mytem.

TRANSLATOR. I could'a' b'in home an hour ago, but for her. Look at me! I've b'in sponging the floor on my hands and knees 'cause'a' her.

SMIEDNIK. (*Sees mop at hatrack; goes to it. He grabs his mop.*) Dawaj! Wy mytem podłoge wustepie kobiat I wtn samotny plazzek tutaj leci na schodach upada na palcach.

TRANSLATOR. I'm mopping the floor in the ladies' room and this maniac here comes running in all stooped over with her finger bent.

SMIEDNIK. Ona widzi mnie I zaczyna płakać. Ja chodzie do niej I chec uspokoic a una mnie voezy nad głowe z moje moitłe.

TRANSLATOR. She sees me and starts sobbing. I go and try to calm her down and she hits me over the head with my mop.

SMIEDNIK. I zamykà mnie wustepie, okolo jedna godzina asstara chinczyka kobieta przychodzie I otwiera dzwi.

TRANSLATOR. Then she locks me in the ladies' room for nearly an hour until an old Chinese woman comes and opens the lock . . .

SMIEDNIK. (*He moves to Wastba.*) Szytyry chas ja ukopnie twoj dzwi. I szytyry chas ty nie otwieraj. Wiedzirs ty jest sztrentny.

TRANSLATOR. Four times I come up here and bang on your door and four times you don't open your door. Don't you know that's nasty?

SMIEDNIK. (*At door.*) Tys scienczie nie jest whop appresivne.

TRANSLATOR. Lucky for you I'm not a violent man. (*He exits, slamming door violently. A pause. Wastba speaks, to Patumiera who starts to pack his things.*)

WASTBA. We are. C'mon, mister, please: we are. We really are. We are . . .

PATUMIERA. (*Repeats softly; gestures "you're nuts" to Wastba first. Perhaps hums a tune, softly. He eyes his belongings; prepares to leave.*) We are.

WASTBA. (*Quietly.*) You are.

PATUMIERA. You are.

WASTBA. They are.

PATUMIERA. They are.

WASTBA. Good morning.

PATUMIERA. Good morning.

WASTBA. How are you?

PATUMIERA. How are you?

WASTBA. I am wonderful. (*Patumiera's flight bags and briefcases are packed. He goes for his jacket.*)

PATUMIERA. I . . . wonderful.

WASTBA. Good.

PATUMIERA. Good.

WASTBA. Too bad . . .

PATUMIERA. Too bad . . .

WASTBA. What happens to women . . . (*Patumiera puts on his suitcoat.*)

PATUMIERA. Wha happens to women . . .

WASTBA. Like us . . .

PATUMIERA. Like us . . .

WASTBA. You are beautiful . . .

PATUMIERA. You . . . beautiful . . .

WASTBA. Debbie . . .

PATUMIERA. Deb . . .
WASTBA. So smart . . .
PATUMIERA. Smart . . .
WASTBA. Not wasting . . .
PATUMIERA. No wasting . . .
WASTBA. Time . . .
PATUMIERA. Time . . . (*Wastba bows her head and sobs.
Patumiera stands, walks to five feet from her and watches, silently.
She looks up and smiles.*)
WASTBA. English . . .
PATUMIERA. English . . .
WASTBA. Is not difficult . . .
PATUMIERA. Is no difficult . . .
WASTBA. Anymore . . .
PATUMIERA. Anymore . . .
WASTBA. Why?
PATUMIERA. Why?
WASTBA. Because . . .
PATUMIERA. Because . . .
WASTBA. Of Debbie . . .
PATUMIERA. Of Debbie . . .
WASTBA. Because of Debbie . . .
PATUMIERA. Because of Debbie . . . (*He smiles at her.*)
WASTBA. Because of Debbie Wastba . . .
PATUMIERA. (*Quietly, to her.*) Because of Debbie Wastba . . .
WASTBA. My teacher . . .
PATUMIERA. My teacher . . .
WASTBA. Who is certainly . . .
PATUMIERA. (*Nearly embracing.*) Who eeis certain . . .
WASTBA. . . . competent.
PATUMIERA. . . . compotentè.
WASTBA. . . . competent.
PATUMIERA. (*Softly, smiling.*) . . . compotentè?
WASTBA. . . . competent.
PATUMIERA. . . . competent? (*Wastba smiles. Nods.*)
WASTBA. Thank you. (*Pauses.*) Good. (*Patumiera smiles.*) It's
hot, huh. (*She wipes her brow.*) I can't breath . . .(*Smiles.*)
PATUMIERA. (*Recognizing the idiom as an old friend.*) Si. Si si.
Si si si.
WASTBA. Huh?

PATUMIERA. (*Pulls at his shirt, mops brow, fans air.*) I canno
. . . breth. (*Smiles.*) I canno breth.
WASTBA. Was that a negative I heard?
PATUMIERA. (*Confused.*) I canno breth?
WASTBA. Mister, this could be the second chance to end all
second chances . . .
PATUMIERA. Scusi?
WASTBA. (*Suddenly.*) Touch the floor!
PATUMIERA. *Managa! l'America! Managa Christophe Columbe!*
(*Makes "you're nuts" gesture.*)
WASTBA. Touch the floor! (*She drops to her knees and touches
the floor.*) I can touch the floor!
PATUMIERA. (*Drops to his knees; touches floor.*) Alora! I cain
tooch the floor . . .
WASTBA. I can touch the desk!
PATUMIERA. Alora! I cain . . . tooch . . . the dest . . .
(*She stands.*)
WASTBA. (*She reaches up to ceiling above her head.*) Can you
touch the ceiling?
PATUMIERA. (*He looks at her desk·and starts to climb onto it.*)
Si . . . é facile.
WASTBA. (*Moves quietly between Patumiera and her desk.*) No
no, now . . . (*Reaches up again.*) Touch the ceiling! Please
mister, I'm begging you. This could be the most important moment
of my life.
PATUMIERA. (*Reaches up to ceiling, but of course, cannot reach
it. Confused, he apologizes, in Italian.*) Signorina . . .
WASTBA. (*Screams; pleading.*) English! Speak English! (*She
reaches again for ceiling.*) Touch the ceiling!
PATUMIERA. *Managa!* I canno . . .
WASTBA. *Say it!*
PATUMIERA. (*Reaching for ceiling, exasperated.*) I canno . . .
I canno tooch the ceiling . . . (*Wastba squeals with delight.*)
WASTBA. (*She takes Patumiera's face in her hands and pulls his
face down to hers.*) God bless you. (*They kiss. Going into the
kiss, Patumiera is confused, thinking he has failed. After the kiss,
he is changed; more confident somehow.*)
PATUMIERA. Tesora . . . (*He reaches for her to kiss her
again.*) Tesorai, mia . . . (*She pulls away from him, realizing.*)
WASTBA. Oh, oh . . .

PATUMIERA. Ey?

WASTBA. (*She grabs his hand and shakes it enthusiastically, carefully holding her body back from his.*) I want to thank you. I really do. I'm really proud. English gets a lot easier, really. Just give it time. (*Pauses.*) You've learned. (*Patumiera suddenly grabs his various bags and briefcases and moves to the door. She backs away. He grabs knob.*) Where are you going? Don't! Don't go! No! *No!!! Don't leave me!*

PATUMIERA. (*Quietly.*) Non ho capito nemmena una parola che tu hai detta. (*Patumiera exits the play, slamming door. Wastba moves to door and leans her back against same. Turns. Locks doors. She pauses a moment. She moves to desk and chair. Music in. She stands facing blackboard. She bows her head. She writes "The Primary English Class" on board and then returns to her desk. She tidies desk top, stacking notebooks, pencils, etc. She places apple center of desk, sits, folds hands on desk behind apple. She weeps. The door opens, Mrs. Pong re-enters, smiles at Wastba.*)

MRS. PONG. (*In Chinese language.*) Hsī wàng méi yòu lòu diào shé mǎ.

TRANSLATOR. I hope I haven't missed anything.

MRS. PONG. (*Burps, touches stomach, embarrassed.*) Wō tsài loú hsià chí lě diǎn dóng hsî. (wǒ) Dù tzǐ gú . . .

TRANSLATOR. I had a little bite to eat downstairs. My stomach is making unforgivable noises. Excuse me.

MRS. PONG. (*In Chinese language.*) . . . lū gū lū dě hsiǎng. Tsēn dùi bū chì . . . Tzì shǎo dūn hái liàng chě. Aň í diàn, bú gùo hái liàng chě.

TRANSLATOR. At least the lights are on. Dim, but on.

MRS. PONG. (*Sits in front row, folds hands, smiles at Wastba. She speaks in Chinese, excitedly.*) Wō mén jì hsǔ niàn bá!

TRANSLATOR. (*Simply.*) Let's go. (*Wastba smiles, hopefully, happily, into Mrs. Pong's hopeful, happy smile.*)

THE LIGHTS FADE TO BLACK.

THE PLAY IS OVER.

NYC — Gloucester, Mass. — NYC,
October, 1974 — March, 1976.
Revised September, 1984.

ADDENDUM

Simultaneous translation is at times wanted.

These points of translation have been carefully selected to establish a vocabulary for the audience, as well as to sustain the presence of the translator's voice.

Such translation should be heard over speakers, in the auditorium. The translators must not be seen by the audience.

Translators' voices should reflect emotional reality of voice being translated, but should be subdued in tone: understated, slightly.

Whenever possible, both a male and female translator should be employed so that sex of translator might match sex of person being translated.

Action should never stop for translation, but should instead slow down, establishing rather a convention than a style.

When the play is performed in translation, which is to say in a non-English-language production, it is suggested that the instructor's role be changed to the language of the country in which the play is being shown and that the object of the class be adapted completely to the learning of that particular language. In certain instances, other characters in the play must be changed to accommodate a changed base language. A straight-forward translation of this play must be avoided in favor of adaptation.

I.H.

DEBORAH WASTBA, *Instructor*
Immersion class #1, 8 p.m. - 8 a.m.
PRIMARY ENGLISH

LESSON PLAN

1. Pleasant welcome and normal chatter.
2. Basic salutations. (Do joke: "The Goods: good morning, good afternoon, good night, good luck, good grief.")
3. Basic customs. (Ours, not theirs.)
4. Short History of English Language. (N.B. Ask in office in a.m.)
5. Lesson #1 from their book. (N.B. Borrow $10 for deposit.)
6. To be: I am, you are, he-she-it is, we are, you are, they are.
7. The concept of "silence." (If NEEDED.)

NOTE:
   a. Collect their slips—check to see if they've paid.
   b. Bring food.
   c. Bring valium, aspirin, etc.
   d. Leave out extra catfood for cats.
   e. Pencils and yellow-lined pads.
   f. Foreign dictionaries?

PROPERTY LIST

Hat rack
Twelve orange student desk/chair units
Orange teacher's desk, with chair
Orange wastebasket
Blackboard and chalk
Pointer
Mop and pail
Brown briefcase, with French/English dictionary ⎫
Black attache case   ⎪
Black duffel bag, with tangerine   ⎬ (Patumiera)
Wristwatch   ⎪
Cigarettes and matches   ⎪
Papers, in mouth   ⎭
Book satchel   ⎫
Brown briefcase, with French/English dictionary ⎪
Umbrella   ⎬ (LaPoubelle)
Cigarettes and matches   ⎪
Papers, in mouth   ⎭
8x10 glossy photo of himself (Patumiera)
Pens, notebooks, books, pads, papers (All)
Briefcases   ⎫
Sacks   ⎪
Papers, in mouth ⎬ (Mulleimer)
Two cameras, with straps ⎭
Box of raisins (Patumiera)
Red apple   ⎫
Several small canvas bags, with books and papers   ⎬ (Yoko)
Papers, in mouth   ⎭
Bookbags, with notebooks, papers, books, "wash 'n dri" ⎫
Shopping bags   ⎪
Handbags   ⎬ (Wastba)
Briefcases   ⎪
Papers, in mouth   ⎭
Four take-out containers, with water (one with tea bag in it)
Bag of candy (LaPoubelle)
Name tag (Mrs. Pong)
Japanese cigarettes (Yoko)
German cigarettes (Mulleimer)
French pipe (LaPoubelle)
Chinese cigarettes (Mrs. Pong)
Dollar bills (All)
Gold make-up case (Yoko)

82

ADDENDUM

The author has requested that the following changes be made in the text of THE PRIMARY ENGLISH CLASS as printed in this edition:

Page 7.
In line 16 of stage-directions, instead of "In dark, we hear Bulgarian folk music." . . . correct to read: "In dark, we hear Translator's Voice, as the history of the Nachsart family is finally revealed."

TRANSLATOR

Once upon a time, 3084 years ago, a powerful family ruled Mesopotamia. Their name was "Nachsart." (*Pauses.*) During the Great Mesopotamian purges, in 1000 B.C., all wealthy families were run out of Mesopotamia by the filthy janitorial class. Most wealthy Mesopotamian families settled in Greece and created the Classics. The Nachsart, a competitive, family of infighters, split up and ventured to all corners of the Earth, creating large, powerful Nations, wherever they settled. (*Pauses.*) Waldo Nachsart, the eldest son, created a smallish nation called Poland. He changed his name to Smiednik. Farook settled Italy, changing his name to Patumiera. Juno, the boring son, settled France, changing his family name to LaPoubelle. The precise one, Fristo, settled Germany, changing the family name there to Mulleimer; while Wanda, the smallest daughter, settled China, changing her name to Pong. Yuna, the outgoing daughter, settled Japan, and changed the family name to Kuzukago. Debba, the greedy daughter, settled the United States of America, changing the family's name there to Wastba. (*Pauses.*) Three thousand years passed without the family ever gathering together, peaceably. Each child's descendants build his or her country into a great world power. And in the year 1984, tonight, in fact, one direct descendant of each Great Nachsart-family child will arrive on the soil of Wastba — in the United States of America — the greatest power of current Western Civilization . . . with one single purpose . . . to learn English language, and fast. (*Pauses.*) Tonight promises to show us a great Family reunion . . . and to give us great insight into the true possibilities of World Peace. (*Smiednik begins to sing.*)

Page 53.
There is a small typo. Insert between "something" and "Nor do I." in Line 2, the following: ". . . something. I have no plan to lose. Nor do I . . ." So, completed line reads: "In this country, it's assumed you're going to lose . . . something. I have no plan to lose. Nor do I. Not at ten dollars a shot."

Pages 57 & 58.
7 lines up from bottom on page 57. CUT all lines after " . . . we have a perfect balance between maniacs and non-maniacs: one-to-one." to page 58, Line 16, LaPoubelle says "Chère mademoiselle . . . etc." Thus, we are cutting Wastba's long story of being molested, so the section now reads, without it: "In this particular city, we have a perfect balance between maniacs and non-maniacs: one-to-one." to which LaPoubelle responds, "(*Quietly. He is completely perplexed.*) Chère mademoiselle . . . écoutez . . . Je suis absolument désolé d'avoir dire ça, mais il faut que vous . . ."

NEW PLAYS

★ **HONOUR by Joanna Murray-Smith.** In a series of intense confrontations, a wife, husband, lover and daughter negotiate the forces of passion, history, responsibility and honour. "HONOUR makes for surprisingly interesting viewing. Tight, crackling dialogue (usually played out in punchy verbal duels) captures characters unable to deal with emotions ... Murray-Smith effectively places her characters in situations that strip away pretense." –*Variety* "... the play's virtues are strong: a distinctive theatrical voice, passionate concerns ... HONOUR might just capture a few honors of its own." –*Time Out Magazine* [1M, 3W] ISBN: 0-8222-1683-3

★ **MR. PETERS' CONNECTIONS by Arthur Miller.** Mr. Miller describes the protagonist as existing in a dream-like state when the mind is "freed to roam from real memories to conjectures, from trivialities to tragic insights, from terror of death to glorying in one's being alive." With this memory play, the Tony Award and Pulitzer Prize-winner reaffirms his stature as the world's foremost dramatist. "... a cross between Joycean stream-of-consciousness and Strindberg's dream plays, sweetened with a dose of William Saroyan's philosophical whimsy ... CONNECTIONS is most intriguing ..." –*The NY Times* [5M, 3W] ISBN: 0-8222-1687-6

★ **THE WAITING ROOM by Lisa Loomer.** Three women from different centuries meet in a doctor's waiting room in this dark comedy about the timeless quest for beauty – and its cost. "... THE WAITING ROOM ... is a bold, risky melange of conflicting elements that is ... terrifically moving ... There's no resisting the fierce emotional pull of the play." –*The NY Times* "... one of the high points of this year's Off-Broadway season ... THE WAITING ROOM is well worth a visit." –*Back Stage* [7M, 4W, flexible casting] ISBN: 0-8222-1594-2

★ **THE OLD SETTLER by John Henry Redwood.** A sweet-natured comedy about two church-going sisters in 1943 Harlem and the handsome young man who rents a room in their apartment. "For all of its decent sentiments, THE OLD SETTLER avoids sentimentality. It has the authenticity and lack of pretense of an Early American sampler." –*The NY Times* "We've had some fine plays Off-Broadway this season, and this is one of the best." –*The NY Post* [1M, 3W] ISBN: 0-8-222-1642-6

★ **LAST TRAIN TO NIBROC by Arlene Hutton.** In 1940 two young strangers share a seat on a train bound east only to find their paths will cross again. "All aboard. LAST TRAIN TO NIBROC is a sweetly told little chamber romance." –*Show Business* "... [a] gently charming little play, reminiscent of Thornton Wilder in its look at rustic Americans who are to be treasured for their simplicity and directness ..." –*Associated Press* "The old formula of boy wins girls, boy loses girl, boy wins girl still works ... [a] well-made play that perfectly captures a slice of small-town-life-gone-by." –*Back Stage* [1M, 1W] ISBN: 0-8222-1753-8

★ **OVER THE RIVER AND THROUGH THE WOODS by Joe DiPietro.** Nick sees both sets of his grandparents every Sunday for dinner. This is routine until he has to tell them that he's been offered a dream job in Seattle. The news doesn't sit so well. "A hilarious family comedy that is even funnier than his long running musical revue *I Love You, You're Perfect, Now Change.*" –*Back Stage* "Loaded with laughs every step of the way." –*Star-Ledger* [3M, 3W] ISBN: 0-8222-1712-0

★ **SIDE MAN by Warren Leight.** 1999 Tony Award winner. This is the story of a broken family and the decline of jazz as popular entertainment. "... a tender, deeply personal memory play about the turmoil in the family of a jazz musician as his career crumbles at the dawn of the age of rock-and-roll ..." –*The NY Times* "[SIDE MAN] is an elegy for two things – a lost world and a lost love. When the two notes sound together in harmony, it is moving and graceful ..." –*The NY Daily News* "An atmospheric memory play ... with crisp dialogue and clearly drawn characters ... reflects the passing of an era with persuasive insight ... The joy and despair of the musicians is skillfully illustrated." –*Variety* [5M, 3W] ISBN: 0-8222-1721-X

DRAMATISTS PLAY SERVICE, INC.
440 Park Avenue South, New York, NY 10016 212-683-8960 Fax 212-213-1539
postmaster@dramatists.com www.dramatists.com

NEW PLAYS

★ **CLOSER by Patrick Marber.** Winner of the 1998 Olivier Award for Best Play and the 1999 New York Drama Critics Circle Award for Best Foreign Play. Four lives intertwine over the course of four and a half years in this densely plotted, stinging look at modern love and betrayal. "CLOSER is a sad, savvy, often funny play that casts a steely, unblinking gaze at the world of relationships and lets you come to your own conclusions ... CLOSER does not merely hold your attention; it burrows into you." *–New York Magazine* "A powerful, darkly funny play about the cosmic collision between the sun of love and the comet of desire." *–Newsweek Magazine* [2M, 2W] ISBN: 0-8222-1722-8

★ **THE MOST FABULOUS STORY EVER TOLD by Paul Rudnick.** A stage manager, headset and prompt book at hand, brings the house lights to half, then dark, and cues the creation of the world. Throughout the play, she's in control of everything. In other words, she's either God, or she thinks she is. "Line by line, Mr. Rudnick may be the funniest writer for the stage in the United States today ... One-liners, epigrams, withering put-downs and flashing repartee: These are the candles that Mr. Rudnick lights instead of cursing the darkness ... a testament to the virtues of laughing ... and in laughter, there is something like the memory of Eden." *–The NY Times* "Funny it is ... consistently, rapaciously, deliriously ... easily the funniest play in town." *–Variety* [4M, 5W] ISBN: 0-8222-1720-1

★ **A DOLL'S HOUSE by Henrik Ibsen, adapted by Frank McGuinness.** Winner of the 1997 Tony Award for Best Revival. "New, raw, gut-twisting and gripping. Easily the hottest drama this season." *–USA Today* "Bold, brilliant and alive." *–The Wall Street Journal* "A thunderclap of an evening that takes your breath away." *–Time Magazine* [4M, 4W, 2 boys] ISBN: 0-8222-1636-1

★ **THE HERBAL BED by Peter Whelan.** The play is based on actual events which occurred in Stratford-upon-Avon in the summer of 1613, when William Shakespeare's elder daughter was publicly accused of having a sexual liaison with a married neighbor and family friend. "In his probing new play, THE HERBAL BED ... Peter Whelan muses about a sidelong event in the life of Shakespeare's family and creates a finely textured tapestry of love and lies in the early 17th-century Stratford." *–The NY Times* "It is a first rate drama with interesting moral issues of truth and expediency." *–The NY Post* [5M, 3W] ISBN: 0-8222-1675-2

★ **SNAKEBIT by David Marshall Grant.** A study of modern friendship when put to the test. "... a rather smart and absorbing evening of water-cooler theater, the intimate sort of Off-Broadway experience that has you picking apart the recognizable characters long after the curtain calls." *–The NY Times* "Off-Broadway keeps on presenting us with compelling reasons for going to the theater. The latest is SNAKEBIT, David Marshall Grant's smart new comic drama about being thirtysomething and losing one's way in life." *–The NY Daily News* [3M, 1W] ISBN: 0-8222-1724-4

★ **A QUESTION OF MERCY by David Rabe.** The Obie Award-winning playwright probes the sensitive and controversial issue of doctor-assisted suicide in the age of AIDS in this poignant drama. "There are many devastating ironies in Mr. Rabe's beautifully considered, piercingly clear-eyed work ..." *–The NY Times* "With unsettling candor and disturbing insight, the play arouses pity and understanding of a troubling subject ... Rabe's provocative tale is an affirmation of dignity that rings clear and true." *–Variety* [6M, 1W] ISBN: 0-8222-1643-4

★ **DIMLY PERCEIVED THREATS TO THE SYSTEM by Jon Klein.** Reality and fantasy overlap with hilarious results as this unforgettable family attempts to survive the nineties. "Here's a play whose point about fractured families goes to the heart, mind – and ears." *–The Washington Post* "... an end-of-the-millennium comedy about a family on the verge of a nervous breakdown ... Trenchant and hilarious ..." *–The Baltimore Sun* [2M, 4W] ISBN: 0-8222-1677-9

DRAMATISTS PLAY SERVICE, INC.
440 Park Avenue South, New York, NY 10016 212-683-8960 Fax 212-213-1539
postmaster@dramatists.com   www.dramatists.com

NEW PLAYS

★ **AS BEES IN HONEY DROWN by Douglas Carter Beane.** Winner of the John Gassner Playwriting Award. A hot young novelist finds the subject of his new screenplay in a New York socialite who leads him into the world of *Auntie Mame* and *Breakfast at Tiffany's*, before she takes him for a ride. "A delicious soufflé of a satire ... [an] extremely entertaining fable for an age that always chooses image over substance." –*The NY Times* "... A witty assessment of one of the most active and relentless industries in a consumer society ... the creation of 'hot' young things, which the media have learned to mass produce with efficiency and zeal." –*The NY Daily News* [3M, 3W, flexible casting] ISBN: 0-8222-1651-5

★ **STUPID KIDS by John C. Russell.** In rapid, highly stylized scenes, the story follows four high-school students as they make their way from first through eighth period and beyond, struggling with the fears, frustrations, and longings peculiar to youth. "In STUPID KIDS ... playwright John C. Russell gets the opera of adolescence to a T ... The stylized teenspeak of STUPID KIDS ... suggests that Mr. Russell may have hidden a tape recorder under a desk in study hall somewhere and then scoured the tapes for good quotations ... it is the kids' insular, ceaselessly churning world, a pre-adult world of Doritos and libidos, that the playwright seeks to lay bare." –*The NY Times* "STUPID KIDS [is] a sharp-edged ... whoosh of teen angst and conformity anguish. It is also very funny." –*NY Newsday* [2M, 2W] ISBN: 0-8222-1698-1

★ **COLLECTED STORIES by Donald Margulies.** From Obie Award-winner Donald Margulies comes a provocative analysis of a student-teacher relationship that turns sour when the protégé becomes a rival. "With his fine ear for detail, Margulies creates an authentic, insular world, and he gives equal weight to the opposing viewpoints of two formidable characters." –*The LA Times* "This is probably Margulies' best play to date ..." –*The NY Post* "... always fluid and lively, the play is thick with ideas, like a stock-pot of good stew." –*The Village Voice* [2W] ISBN: 0-8222-1640-X

★ **FREEDOMLAND by Amy Freed.** An overdue showdown between a son and his father sets off fireworks that illuminate the neurosis, rage and anxiety of one family – and of America at the turn of the millennium. "FREEDOMLAND's more obvious links are to *Buried Child* and *Bosoms and Neglect*. Freed, like Guare, is an inspired wordsmith with a gift for surreal touches in situations grounded in familiar and real territory." –*Curtain Up* [3M, 4W] ISBN: 0-8222-1719-8

★ **STOP KISS by Diana Son.** A poignant and funny play about the ways, both sudden and slow, that lives can change irrevocably. "There's so much that is vital and exciting about STOP KISS ... you want to embrace this young author and cheer her onto other works ... the writing on display here is funny and credible ... you also will be charmed by its heartfelt characters and up-to-the-minute humor." –*The NY Daily News* "... irresistibly exciting ... a sweet, sad, and enchantingly sincere play." –*The NY Times* [3M, 3W] ISBN: 0-8222-1731-7

★ **THREE DAYS OF RAIN by Richard Greenberg.** The sins of fathers and mothers make for a bittersweet elegy in this poignant and revealing drama. "... a work so perfectly judged it heralds the arrival of a major playwright ... Greenberg is extraordinary." –*The NY Daily News* "Greenberg's play is filled with graceful passages that are by turns melancholy, harrowing, and often, quite funny." –*Variety* [2M, 1W] ISBN: 0-8222-1676-0

★ **THE WEIR by Conor McPherson.** In a bar in rural Ireland, the local men swap spooky stories in an attempt to impress a young woman from Dublin who recently moved into a nearby "haunted" house. However, the tables are soon turned when she spins a yarn of her own. "You shed all sense of time at this beautiful and devious new play." –*The NY Times* "Sheer theatrical magic. I have rarely been so convinced that I have just seen a modern classic. Tremendous." –*The London Daily Telegraph* [4M, 1W] ISBN: 0-8222-1706-6

DRAMATISTS PLAY SERVICE, INC.
440 Park Avenue South, New York, NY 10016 212-683-8960 Fax 212-213-1539
postmaster@dramatists.com www.dramatists.com